# Clean Eating

## 15-Minute Clean Eating Recipes

## Meals that Improve Your Health, Make You Lean, and Boost Your Metabolism!

## - Second Edition -

JASON GREEN

# CONTENTS

Introduction                                                              i

Chapter 1: Food and Your Health

Chapter 2: The Road to Healthy and Clean Eating        6

Chapter 3: Quick n' Easy Breakfast Recipes        10

5-Minute Strawberry Chia Pudding

Fruits, Nuts, and Oats Jar

Avocados and Toast

Salmon and Egg Breakfast Muffin

5-Minute Egg Bowl

Mexican Breakfast

No-Sweat Blueberry and Oats Muffin

Vegetable Hash with Poached Eggs

Farm Veggies with Romesco Sauce

Oatmeal Power Bowl

Egg-In-The-Hole

Vanilla-Almond Chia Pudding

Skinny Omelet

Apple Mug Muffin

Simple Tofu Quiche

Cake Batter Chia Pudding with Coconut Whipped Cream

Banana Bread Breakfast Cookies

Instant Avocado Toast

Fruit and Nuts Oatmeal

Leafy Breakfast Skillet

Spinach and Cheese Omelet

Egg and Cheese Breakfast Waffle

Oatmeal Muffins on the Go

No-Cook Clean Eating Breakfast Bowl

No-Guilt Pudding

Mixed Berries and Cottage Cheese

Chapter 4: Easy Whip Delicious and Healthy Meals          49

Not Your Average Tuna Sandwich

Classic Seared Salmon

Steak and Potatoes Plate

Bow Tie Pasta and Veggie Salad

Refreshing Salad

Shrimp in Angel Hair Pasta

Broiled Asian Salmon

Quinoa Salad with Asparagus, Dates, and Orange

Fennel and Spinach Salad with Shrimp and Balsamic Vinaigrette

Oven-Fried Sweet Potatoes

Crab Salad-Stuffed Eggs

Arugula, Grape, and Sunflower Seed Salad

Carrot Soup with Yogurt

Nutty Warm Brussels Sprouts Salad

Seared Tuna Niçoise

Minty Millet & Pomegranate Salad

Shrimp and Avocado Summer Rolls

Chapter 5 – Dinner for Motivation                    75

Chicken with Brussels Sprouts and Mustard Sauce

Lemony Chicken Kebabs with Tomato Parsley Salad

Tenderloin Steaks with Red Onion Marmalade

Peppercorn Crusted Beef Tenderloin with Gremolata

Arctic Char with Orange-Caper Relish

Grilled Pork Chops with Two-Melon Salsa

Tuna Scaloppini with Onion, Mint, and Almond Topping

Avocado and Quinoa Stuffed Acorn Squash

Cauliflower Risotto

Harissa Chicken Stuffed Eggplant

Grilled Chicken on Zucchini Noodles

Wild Rice Fry on Baked Zucchini

Quinoa and Berries Salad

Shrimp and Spinach Salad

Zesty Chicken Bake

5-Ingredient Grilled Chicken

Broiled Steak Sirloin

Seared Tuna and Veggies

Grilled Chops with Refreshing Salsa

Arugula Salad in Tahini Dressing

Chapter 6: Healthy and Delicious Snacks and Shakes You Can          110
Make in a Breeze

Belly Busting Pomegranate and Berry Smoothie

Spiced Green Smoothie

Refreshing Smoothie

Peanut Butter and Apple Snacks

No-Bake Energy Bars

Lettuce Wraps

Kale Chips

Chile Lime and Maple Cinnamon Kettle Corn

Gooey Mac & Cheese Balls

Sweet and Sticky Popcorn Balls

Peanut Butter Yogurt Dip

Classic Cucumber and Tomato Salad

Baked Apple Chips

Ranch Dip

Sweet Potato Hummus

Chili Lime Spiced Pumpkin Seeds

Sweet and Spicy Pecans

Quinoa Salad with a Zing

Homemade Trail Mix

Apple Sandwich

Low-Cal Tuna Salad

Mixed Greens Salad

Asian Broccoli Salad

Kale and Beet Salad

Sweet and Savory Salad

Cabbage Salad

Watermelon Salad

Chapter 7 – Tasty Desserts                                  143

Mocha Cashew Bars

Chocolate Peanut Squares

Lemon, Coconut and Cayenne Mousse

Date and Cashew Protein Balls

Chestnut Crusted Cheesecake with Cranberry Sauce

Individual Apple and Pecan Crumbles

Buttermilk Plum Cake

Chapter 8 – More Delicious Shakes and Smoothies            155

Sunshine on a Cup

Spiced Apple Shake

Coco-Banana Green Shake

Kale and Berry Shake

Berrilicious Quinoa Smoothie

Pomegranate Smoothie

Clean Eating Green Shake

Conclusion                                                    162

# Introduction

Are you tired of hearing people say, "I think you're gaining weight?" Do you wish you could fit into your favorite jeans again? Or are you just looking for ways to be healthy, starting with your diet? This book can help you with that!

We all know that a healthy lifestyle is key to maintaining a healthy weight and preventing chronic diseases, such as stroke, diabetes, and cancer; however, most people opt to lead sedentary lifestyles and consume junk foods rich in cholesterol, salt, sugar, and fats that are all bad for the health.

In this age where most people don't have time to prepare healthy meals, much more exercise, who has the time to lead a healthy lifestyle, right? Wrong! Even if you're too busy juggling your responsibilities at work and home, it's still vital that you maintain a healthy diet and at least have regular physical activity.

What's the danger of an unhealthy lifestyle? First, it can cause you to become overweight or obese. In fact, according to the World Health Organization (WHO), the prevalence of overweight and obese people all over the world is on the rise. In 2014, WHO reported that 1.9 billion adults (18 years old and above) were overweight and of this number, 600 million individuals were obese. The prevalence of these health problems has more than doubled since 1980. What's even more alarming is that even children suffer from obesity and being overweight. In 2013, WHO reported that 42 million children 5 years old and below were either obese or overweight. Health experts agree that the cause of these health problems are increased consumption of foods high in fat and low in nutrition, as well as lack in physical activity.

Being overweight or obese was noted to be the cause of more deaths all over the world compared to being underweight; this means that these health issues should be taken seriously. That's because weighing more than what is recommended for your Body Mass Index (BMI) puts you at risk of developing more serious health problems, such as hypertension, stroke, coronary heart disease, type 2 diabetes, some types of cancer, and more. Children who are obese have been seen to have higher risks of developing the same diseases and even premature death.

The good news is that being obese or overweight can be prevented through a healthy and clean diet and exercise. Since diet is the most important factor in order to improve health and lose weight, you should focus on the meals that you consume. Most would think that skipping meals is the best way to cut down calories and shed fat, but this could lead to even more health problems. What you need to do is to stick to the recommended daily caloric intake (2,500 Kcal for men and 2,000 Kcal for women) to maintain your ideal weight by choosing the best type of foods to make up your daily caloric consumption. Of course, your best choices for your meals are fresh fruits and vegetables, lean proteins, and whole grains.

Like I said, a busy schedule is never an excuse to not maintain a healthy diet; that's because you can prepare healthy meals for you and your family in a breeze with the help of this book!

Before I go on any further, I'd like to thank you and congratulate you for downloading this book, "15-Minute Clean Eating Recipes: Meals that Improve Your Health, Make You Lean, and Boost Your Metabolism!"

This book contains delicious and healthy recipes for breakfast, lunch, dinner, snacks and shakes that will help you achieve your health goals. You don't even have to spend much time in the kitchen because these recipes can be cooked in 15 minutes or less, perfect for busy individuals like you!

There is also a chapter that will help you learn the benefits of clean eating and how important diet is for your overall health. Finally, there is also a part of this book that provides tips to help you successfully begin a lifestyle of clean eating.

Begin your journey today! Improve your health, become leaner, and boost your metabolism through clean eating!

# Chapter 1: Food and Your Health

We all know that the food we eat is central to our health.
Consuming nutritious food can help improve our metabolism
and prevent chronic diseases, while consuming too much food
that has less or zero nutrition could lead to weight gain,
undernourishment, and could even increase the risk of
developing serious health conditions.

The food we eat contains nutrients; these nutrients allow the
cells found in our body to perform their functions well. These
nutrients also allow the body to grow and develop. Having a diet
that doesn't contain the nutrients it needs could lead to a
disruption in your bodily functions, such as a slow-down in the
body's metabolic processes, which could lead to weight gain.

Unfortunately, people today would rather eat fast food or
microwavable dinners instead of preparing healthy meals in their
kitchen. They would rather give into to their cravings and satisfy
their hunger pangs with comfort food, instead of choosing
nutrition-dense foods that will not only satiate them, but will also
provide the vitamins and minerals that are essential to the body.
What people don't realize is although these foods satisfy their
cravings and make them feel full, it's all nothing but junk—high
in calories, rich in unhealthy fats and sugar, but low in nutrients.

Although an occasional splurging into junk food won't absolutely affect your health, consistently being on a diet of mostly of empty calorie foods (foods that have calories mostly from fats or added sugars), a.k.a. junk food, can ultimately lead to serious health problems. Numerous researches and studies conclude that most health problems today are all related to having a poor diet. Some of the effects on health of an unhealthy diet are:

- **Nutritional Deficiency**- Most people today lack the nutrients that their body needs leading to different health complications.

  Nutritionist Dr. Steven Masley wrote in one of his articles that the average diet in the US (mostly made up of high processed foods) is deficient in fiber, omega-3 fatty acids, calcium, and magnesium.

  Fiber is important to the body to maintain a healthy digestive system and to maintain healthy cholesterol and blood sugar levels. *You can, however, prevent nutritional deficiency by consuming healthy foods and eating good sources of fiber such as fruits, vegetables, and whole grains.*

- **Weight Gain**- As we all know, junk food contains loads of calories, but did you know how many calories you're eating in a single burger meal? If you're eating a McDonald's Big Mac (563Kcal), medium fries (383 Kcal), and medium vanilla shake (777 Kcal), that means you're consuming 1,680 calories in just a single meal.

  However, if you consume a meal made of half of roasted chicken breast (142 Kcal), a medium-sized baked potato (130 Kcal), with half a cup of green peas (67 Kcal) on the side, you're only consuming 339 calories, which is lesser in calories than a single serving of medium fries, and it is even more nutritious.

Like I said earlier, the recommended daily calories for men are 2,500 and 2,000 for women. Consuming 500 calories above the recommended amount could lead you to gain one pound per week. This means if you eat fast food meals (1,700 average calories per meal) for lunch and dinner, you're already consuming an excess of 900-1,400 calories in those two meals alone!

*But again, I'd like you to remember that calories are not your enemies. Your body needs calories for energy, however, what you need to watch out for are foods that are calorie rich, but lack nutrients.*

- **Cardiovascular Diseases**- Pizza, burgers, fries, and other junk foods contain processed fats, such as saturated fat, trans fat, and cholesterol, that could lead to developing heart disease. These foods, along with processed foods contain excessive sodium are also linked to an increased risk of having hypertension and stroke.

  *Like calories, most people believe that fats are the villains when they are trying to eat healthy or lose weight. However, what you need to understand is that the body needs the healthy type of fats in order to aid the absorption of some vitamins (vitamins A, E, D, and K) in the body. Some examples of healthy fats are polyunsaturated fat (omega-3 fatty acids) and monounsaturated fat.*

- **Increased Risk of Type 2 Diabetes**- Processed foods, junk foods, and other high glycemic index foods are not only rich in calories and harmful fats, but they also contain large amounts of processed carbohydrates. A diet rich in in carbs can cause spikes in blood sugar levels, which could eventually develop into type 2 diabetes.

    *Like other lifestyle related diseases, insulin resistance, and type 2 diabetes can be prevented through weight loss and a healthy diet made up of vegetables, fruits, while grain, fish, and lean meats.*

Knowing that your usual diet can eventually cause you to develop certain health problems like the ones I mentioned above, it's just about time that you start the clean eating lifestyle. Unlike the other fad diets today, this lifestyle has a simple concept of choosing all-natural, unprocessed, whole foods, while limiting or totally eliminating refined and processed foods. A balanced meal of protein, carbohydrates, and fat is also encouraged in clean eating, while watching out for fat, sugar, and salt (which most processed food contains).

By avoiding harmful toxins and excessive fat, calories, sugar, and sodium, clean eating is sure to provide plenty of health benefits; some of the benefits are:

- **Improved Energy**- A healthy diet that contains nutrients such as B complex vitamins and iron provides you fuel and an extra boost of energy that you need for the day. You are also able to avoid foods that spike your sugar levels and cause you to feel fatigue.

Clean eating is perfect for adults who need to balance their work and life at home. By serving a fiber-rich breakfast, you will be given a surge of energy that will last through lunch.

- **Boosts Metabolism**-A clean eating lifestyle encourages you to eat five to six small meals every day; doing this will make your metabolism work on high throughout the day. Other than this, clean eating also includes a diet that consists of complex carbohydrates and lean protein that balances the metabolism and also maintains healthy levels of insulin.

- **Good for the Heart**- Clean eating also means consuming foods that are rich in healthy fats that combats harmful cholesterol levels that lowers your risk of developing cardio vascular diseases.

- **Supports Mental Health**- A diet that consists of fish, lean meat, healthy fat (olive oil, avocado, nuts), and fruits and veggies, are found to help maintain the brain's health and also prevent cognitive decline.

- **Prevents Cancer**- Numerous studies show that consistently consuming processed foods (which are rich in saturated fat) increases your risk of developing cancer. Clean eating that encourages you to eat vegetables and fruits and increases your consumption of antioxidants and phytonutrients that help prevent cancer.

- **Improve Your Mood**-A study from New Zealand found that a diet rich in fruits and vegetables can help improve one's mood and increases a feeling of happiness.

- **Gives the Skin a Natural Glow**- Following a nutritious diet not only makes you healthy, but the vitamins and minerals from your diet also give you a natural, healthy glow.

I hope you're excited to start this new type of lifestyle after learning about the clean eating lifestyle and how it can contribute to your health and also allow you to lose weight. Again, even with a busy schedule, or even if you're just a beginner in healthy eating, clean eating is for you! Learn how you can successfully achieve this lifestyle in the next chapter!

# Chapter 2: The Road to Healthy and Clean Eating

Leading a lifestyle of clean eating and enjoying its full benefits all relies on how you prepare for it. It is vital that from the beginning you are committed and armed with knowledge of how to properly follow the clean eating lifestyle. To help you with that, I have listed a couple of tips below as you begin your journey on the road to healthy and clean eating.

1. **Do a Pantry Purge**- Your goal for clean eating is to minimize or eliminate your consumption of processed foods and refined foods as much as possible. In order to follow this easily and avoid the temptation of giving into unhealthy foods, one of the things that you have to do is to raid your pantry and throw away (or donate to charity) any type of food that is not all natural, unprocessed, and unrefined. Clear out your cabinets, fridge and pantry; take this opportunity to also organize your stocks.

2. **Go Shopping**- When you're done clearing your pantry, you might want to consider re-stocking; this time, choose ingredients and food items that are clean eating friendly.

   Here is a basic list of clean eating foods you have to

have in your pantry:

- **Fruits and Vegetables**- Purchase as many vegetables and fruits that you will need for the week or two. You can choose to opt for organic produce too, but what's most important is that you have a variety of fresh products in your pantry (the more color you have on your plate, the better).

- **Beans and Legumes**- These are a great source of protein, plus you can even buy canned ones so you can easily stock them in your pantry. Just remember to choose low-sodium varieties or those that have no sugar added in them.

- **Fish Rich in Omega-3**-For a good source of the "good fat," the best choices for your meals are fatty fish like salmon, herring, tuna, and mackerel.

- **Lean Meats**- Other than beans and legumes, another source of protein that you can opt for are lean meats. Go for chicken breasts instead of thighs, beef and pork is fine, as long as you stick with the lean cuts. You can also stock organic eggs your healthy breakfasts.

- **Whole Grain and Wheat**- Brown rice, whole-wheat bread, whole-grain cereals, old-fashioned oatmeal, whole-grain pasta, and quinoa are some of the best examples of whole and whole-wheat foods. These foods are a great source of fiber which prevents sugar levels to spike, it is good for digestion, and will make you feel full for longer periods of time; which can also help you lose weight.

- **Nuts and Seeds**- These foods are not only great for snack time, but are also a good ingredient in adding texture to your dishes. Nuts like almonds and walnuts, and seeds such as flax seeds and chia seeds are rich in omega-3 fatty acids and other types of good fats.

- **Herbs and Spices**- Never think that clean eating means consuming bland meals. In fact, you can choose to use any herbs and spices in your meals.

- **Oils**- Again, you still need fats to obtain a balanced meal, and you also need oils for cooking; however, you should be wise on choosing healthier options, such as extra virgin olive oil, coconut oil, almond oil, and walnut oil.

- **Sweeteners**- Since clean eating involves eliminating processed food, this means that you also have say goodbye to processed sugar. To add sweetness to your dishes and beverages, the best options to stock in your pantry are honey, stevia, coconut palm sugar, and maple syrup.

- **Beverages**- Of course, water is still your best bet as beverage when you're leading a clean eating lifestyle. You can also consume unsweetened green tea, coconut water, low fat or skim milk, soymilk, coconut milk, and almond milk.

- **Others**- Condiments such as balsamic vinegar, low-sodium ketchup (or preferably homemade), hot sauce, and sugar-free mustard are clean eating friendly. You can also use all-natural peanut butter on your sandwiches and snacks, as it is a good source of protein.

3.  **Make Sure You Have a Well-Balanced Meal**- Most people today have diets that are rich in carbs and fat and lacks in protein. In making your meals make sure that you have the right servings for protein, carbs, and healthy fat.

4.  **Learn to Read Labels**- You don't have to be a nutrition expert to learn how to read labels, but at least be wary of the contents that the food you buy has. Always watch out for how many fats (and what type), salts, and sugars the food you're buying has. Also, a good rule of thumb is to always avoid products that have ingredients that look like more of a science experiment (full of additives and chemicals).

5.  **Quit Drinking Your Calories**- Even if you cut down on your meal consumption to limit your calories, if you consume soft drinks, coffee, and frappes, you're still prone of consuming more calories than you think. That's because these beverages are high in calories. So it's best to stick with the beverages listed down in number 2.

6.  **Eat Five to Six Meals a Day**- To avoid the unnecessary cravings and overeating, it is recommended to divide your meals into five to six times a day. Start your day with breakfast, and then have a light snack before having lunch. Eat light snacks again in the late afternoon before having a healthy dinner.

7.  **Exercise**- Besides having a healthy diet and leading a clean eating lifestyle, it's still best to have a regular physical activity at least 30 minutes every day. If you have a busy schedule after breakfast, what I recommend you to do is to wake up 30-40 minutes earlier for exercise. Or you could simply vow to skip using the elevator to your office and use the stairs instead as a form of daily physical activity.

Are you excited to start cooking quick and easy clean eating meals? Turn to the next page to see the recipes!

# Chapter 3: Quick n' Easy Breakfast Recipes

If you're dead serious about following the clean eating lifestyle, then you must also commit to having breakfast every single day. If you find your mornings too busy to cook meals, what I suggest you do is to wake up a few minutes earlier to prepare your meals. That's because healthy breakfasts need not take so much time in cooking and preparing them; in fact, you can even make ones less than 15 minutes! The secret for some of the recipes is to prepare the ingredients you'll need the night before, or prep your food as takeaways that you can bring in your workplace.

## *5-Minute Strawberry Chia Pudding*

Prep time: 5 minutes (needs to be prepared the night before)

Ingredients:

3 tbsp. chia seeds

½ cup almond milk

¼ cup low-fat yogurt

½ lemon juice

¼ tsp. lemon zest

2 tsp. honey

½ cup frozen strawberries (sliced)


## Procedure

1. Pour the almond milk in a mason jar, or any glass container with a lid, and mix it together with the lemon juice, honey, and yogurt.

2. Add the lemon zest and chia seeds, mix to make a pudding, cover, and leave in the fridge to chill overnight.

3. In the morning, take out the pudding and top with frozen strawberry slices before consuming.

You Lean, and Boost Your Metabolism!

## *Fruits, Nuts, and Oats Jar*

Prep time: 15 minutes (needs to be prepared the night before)

Ingredients:

¼ cup quick-cooking oats

1/3 cup almond milk

½ cup 2% Greek yogurt

¼ cup blueberries

¼ cup banana slices

¼ cup ripe mango chunks

3 tbsp. mixed nuts (unsalted)

Procedure

1. Place the quick-cooking oats first in a mason jar, or any glass container with a lid, and mix thoroughly with the almond milk.

2. Top the oats with yogurt, followed by the mixed fruits and nuts.

3. Cover and leave in the fridge to chill overnight.

4. You can eat it as it is in the morning, or soak the lower part of the jar (the one with oats) in hot water so the oats are warm before consuming them.

## *Avocados and Toast*

Prep time: 10-12 minutes

Ingredients:

1 medium-sized avocado

2 slices whole-wheat bread

1 tsp. lemon or lime juice

2 whole eggs (preferably organic)

salt and pepper to taste

chili flakes (optional)

Procedure

1. Toast your bread.

2. While waiting for your bread, cut the avocado into half and throw away the pit. Scoop the avocado meat and place it in a small bowl. Mash the avocado and season it with salt and pepper. Add the lemon juice to the mash and mix well. Set aside.

3. Heat up a non-stick pan and make sunny side up eggs

4. Spread the avocado mash on top of each of the toasted bread, and then top each slice with the cooked eggs. You can sprinkle chili flakes to add flavor and heat on your breakfast.

5. Consume immediately or wrap it to go to eat them on your way to the office.

## *Salmon and Egg Breakfast Muffin*

Prep time: 15 minutes

Ingredients:

1 or 2 slice/s of smoked salmon

1 whole wheat toasted English muffin

½ tbsp. coconut oil

1 tbsp. onion (minced)

1 egg (preferably organic)

1 slice tomato

salt to taste

Procedure

1. Drizzle oil in pan heated over medium fire. Sauté the onions for 1-2 minutes.

2. Beat the egg, and add it to the pan with the onion. Season with salt, and cook for about 30-40 seconds.

3. Cut the toasted English muffin in half. Place the tomato slice, followed by the egg, and top with the smoked salmon slices.

# 5-Minute Egg Bowl

Prep time: 5 minutes

Ingredients:

2 eggs (preferably organic)

2 tbsp. unsweetened almond milk

1 stalk green onion (diced)

2 tbsp. low-fat cheddar (shredded)

1 small tomato (roughly chopped)

a pinch of cayenne

salt to taste

Procedure

1. Beat the eggs in a microwavable bowl (or a ramekin), and season with cayenne pepper and salt. Add the milk and diced green onions; stir well.

2. Place the bowl in the microwave and cook on high for 45 seconds. Take the bowl out and stir using a fork.

3. Place back in the microwave and cook for another 45 seconds.

4. While still hot, stir in the shredded cheddar with the eggs and cover using a clean paper towel. Let it sit for a minute to allow the cheese to melt.

5. Top with the chopped tomato before serving.

## *Mexican Breakfast*

Prep time: 8 minutes

Ingredients:

1 pc. whole-wheat tortilla (slightly toasted)

2 eggs (preferably organic)

¼ cup black beans (rinse and drain first)

2 tbsp. low or no-sodium salsa

2 tbsp. low-fat cheddar (shredded)

½ tbsp. olive oil

Procedure

1. Heat oil in a pan over medium fire. Scramble the eggs, and pour in the pan.

2. Before the egg sets, add the black beans to the pan and stir well. Set aside.

3. To assemble, lay the tortilla on a plate and add the eggs and beans; top with cheddar and salsa. Roll like a burrito and slice into half.

# No-Sweat Blueberry and Oats Muffin

Prep time: 4-5 minutes

## Ingredients:

¼ cup quick-cooking oats

1 whole egg (preferably organic)

1-cup blueberries

1 tsp. liquid stevia

1 tbsp. almond milk

## Procedure

1. Mix all the ingredients in a microwave oven-safe mug. Stir well.

2. Cook in the microwave on high for about 1-1.5 minutes. Watch the muffin closely, as it may overflow.

3. When the muffin is firm, turn the mug upside down on a plate to transfer the muffin. Let it cool for a bit before consuming.

## *Vegetable Hash with Poached Eggs*
*Serves:* 4

### Ingredients

- 4 Tsp. Olive Oil
- 1 C. Chopped Vidalia Or Other Sweet Onion
- 1 C. Sliced Fingerling Or Small Red Potatoes
- 1 Tsp. Dried Herbes De Provence
- 1 C. Chopped Zucchini
- 1 C. Chopped Yellow Squash
- 1 C. Green Beans, Trimmed And Cut Into ½-Inch Pieces
- ½ Tsp. Kosher Salt
- ½ Tsp. Freshly Ground Black Pepper, Divided
- 2 C. Chopped Seeded Tomato
- 2 Tbsp. Sliced Chives
- 2 Tbsp. Chopped Fresh Flat-Leaf Parsley
- 1 Tbsp. White Vinegar
- 4 Eggs
- 1 Oz. Parmesan Cheese, Shredded

### Procedure

1. Heat a skillet over high heat and add the oil. Swirl it to coat. Sauté the potatoes, onion, and Herbes de Provence. Spread this out into a single layer in the

pan and cook for four minutes without stirring, or until the potatoes have lightly browned.

2. Reduce the heat to medium and stir in the squash, zucchini, salt, beans, and three-eighths of a teaspoon of pepper. Sauté for three minutes and then remove the pan from the heat. Cover and allow it to rest for five minutes. Stir in the chives, tomato, and parsley.

3. Add some water to the skillet, filling it two-thirds of the way full, and bring it to a boil. Reduce the heat and simmer it. Stir in the vinegar and break each egg into its own custard cup. Gently pour the eggs into the pan and cook them for three minutes or until they reached your desired doneness. Carefully remove the eggs with a slotted spoon.

4. Divide the squash amongst four plates and top the servings with an egg. Sprinkle with the last of the pepper and the parmesan cheese.

# Farm Veggies with Romesco Sauce

*Serves:* 4

## Ingredients

- 4-6 Fresh Eggs
- 1 C. Fire-Roasted Tomatoes, Crushed
- 1 Clove Garlic, Crushed
- 1 C. Roasted Red Peppers, Drained
- ½ C. Raw Slivered Almonds
- Salt
- 2 Tsp. Paprika
- 1 Tsp. Cayenne Pepper
- Carrots
- Asparagus
- Brussels Sprouts
- Onion
- White Sweet Potatoes
- Spinach
- 1 Tbsp. Extra-Virgin Olive Oil
- Salt

## Procedure

1. Preheat your oven to 400 degrees Fahrenheit.
2. Clean and chop the vegetables.
3. Line the vegetables on a baking sheet and sprinkle them with oil and a little salt. Mix them up to coat.

4. Roast them for forty minutes or until they're tender.
5. As you roast the vegetables, combine the fire roasted tomatoes through the cayenne pepper together in a food processor and pulse until it's thick. Pour it into a bowl and set it aside in the refrigerator until you're ready to serve.
6. Poach the eggs by filling a pot with two cups of water and a tablespoon of vinegar. Crack the eggs into a ramekin individually. Once the water starts to boil, stir it with a spatula until it begins to move in a circular motion gently.
7. Slowly pour the egg into the water and use the spatula to move it together if it starts to separate.
8. Allow it to poach for three to four minutes and spoon it out onto a plate. Set it aside and finish the rest.
9. When the vegetables are finished cooking, transfer them to a serving platter and serve them with the eggs and sauce.

## *Oatmeal Power Bowl*

*Serves:* 1

Ingredients

- 1 Banana, Mashed
- 2 Tbsp. Chia Seeds
- ⅓ C. Rolled Oats
- ¼ Tsp. Cinnamon
- ⅔ C. Almond Milk
- ⅓ C. Water
- 1 Tbsp. Ground Flax
- Pepita Seeds
- Cinnamon
- Nut Butter

Procedure

1. The evening before, mash the banana in a bowl until its smooth and stir in the chia, cinnamon, oats, milk, and water until it's combined. Cover and refrigerate the mixture overnight.
2. In the morning, scoop it into a medium pot and increase the heat to high. Bring it to a simmer and then reduce the heat to low and stir until it's heated through and thickened. Stir in the flax.
3. Pour into a bowl and then garnish with the last three ingredients.

# Egg-In-The-Hole

*Serves:* 6

## Ingredients

- 2 Acorn Squash
- 6 Eggs
- 2 Tbsp. Extra-Virgin Olive Oil
- Salt And Pepper To Taste
- 6 Pitted Dates
- 8 Walnut Halves
- Fresh Parsley

## Procedure

1. . Preheat your oven to 375 degrees Fahrenheit.
2. Slice the squash crosswise to get three slices with holes in the center. They should be around ¾" thick.
3. Remove the seeds and put the slices on a baking sheet lined with parchment paper. Sprinkle it with salt and pepper and bake for twenty minutes.
4. As the squash bakes put the walnuts and dates on a cutting board and chop until they look like coarse sand.
5. Take the squash out and drizzle the slices with olive oil.
6. Crack an egg into the center of each slice and sprinkle with salt and pepper. Sprinkle the date and walnut mixture over the surface of the squash and eggs.

7. Return them to the oven for eight to ten minutes or until the eggs reach your desired doneness.
8. Garnish with the parsley and serve.
9. Drizzle with some maple syrup if you like.

# Vanilla-Almond Chia Pudding

*Serves:* 2

## Ingredients

- 2 C. Unsweetened Almond Milk
- ½ C. Chia Seeds
- ½ Tsp. Vanilla Extract
- 2 Tbsp. Pure Maple Syrup
- Fruit For Topping
- Almonds To Garnish

## Procedure

1. Combine the milk with the chia seeds, sweetener, and vanilla in a bowl. Mix until it's combined and the mixture looks thick. Store it in the refrigerator covered overnight or at least for an hour.
2. Stir it before you serve and add a bit of water to it if it's too thick. Top with the fruits and nuts.

## *Skinny Omelet*

*Serves:* 1

### Ingredients

- 2 Eggs
- ⅛ Tsp. Sea Salt
- 2 Tbsp. Of Chopped Chives
- 3 Tbsp. Pesto
- 2 Oz. Goat Cheese Or Feta
- 1 C. Mixed Salad Greens

### Procedure

1. Beat the eggs and salt in a bowl.
2. IN a skillet over medium heat, pour the egg mix in and swirl it so it spread out thin across the pan.
3. Sprinkle the eggs with chives and allow them to set.
4. Run a spatula under the omelet and slide it out from the pan onto a cutting board.
5. Spread the pesto across the service and sprinkle it with the salad greens and cheese. Begin with one end and roll it away from you and cut it in half on the diagonal. Season it with some salt and pepper and serve with some chopped chives as a garnish.

# Apple Mug Muffin

*Serves:* 1

## Ingredients

- 1 Tbsp. Grass Fed Butter
- 2 Tbsp. Unsweetened Applesauce
- 1 Egg
- ¼ Tsp. Vanilla
- 1 Tsp. Maple Syrup
- 3 Tbsp. Almond Flour
- ½ Tsp. Cinnamon
- Pinch Of Salt
- ⅛ Tsp. Baking Powder
- 1 Tbsp. Apple, Minced
- ⅛ Tsp. Crumbled Walnuts
- ⅛ Tsp. Cold Butter

## Procedure

1. Melt the butter in the microwave in a mug on low power.
2. Whisk the applesauce, vanilla, egg, and syrup until it's combined.
3. Add the almond meal, baking powder, cinnamon, and salt and stir for half a minute.
4. Add the apple, crumbled walnuts, and cold butter. Microwave it for one minute and allow it to cool.

# *Simple Tofu Quiche*
*Serves:* 8

## Ingredients

- 3 Medium Potatoes
- 2 Tbsp. Melted Butter
- ¼ Tsp. Salt And Pepper
- 12.3 Oz. Extra Firm Silken Tofu, Patted Dry
- 2 Tbsp. Nutritional Yeast
- 3 Tbsp. Hummus
- Sea Salt And Black Pepper
- 3 Garlic Cloves, Chopped
- 2 Leeks, Sliced
- ¾ C. Cherry Tomatoes, Halved
- 1 C. Chopped Broccoli

## Procedure

1. Preheat your oven to 450 degrees Fahrenheit and spritz a nine and a half inch pie pan with cooking spray.
2. Grate the potatoes and measure out three cups. Then transfer it to a clean paper towel and squeeze out any excess moisture. Add this to the pie dish and drizzle it with melted butter and a quarter of a teaspoon of salt and pepper. Toss it to coat and then use your fingers to press it into the pan and up the sides to make an even layer.

3. Bake it for twenty-five minutes or until it's golden brown all over. Set it aside.
4. As the crust bakes, prepare the vegetables and the garlic. Add them to a baking sheet and toss them with two tablespoons of olive oil and a pinch of salt and pepper. Toss them to coat. Put them in the oven with the crust. When you take out the crust, lower the heat to 400 degrees and keep baking the vegetables until they're soft and golden brown, around half an hour. Lower the oven temperature to 375 degrees and set the vegetables aside.
5. Add the tofu to a food processor with the hummus, yeast, and a quarter of a teaspoon of salt and pepper. Pulse and then set it aside.
6. Remove the vegetables from the oven and add them to a mixing bowl. Top them with the tofu mixture. Toss it to coat and add the mixture to the crust. Spread it into an even layer.
7. Bake it at 375 degrees for half an hour or until the top appears golden brown. If the crust gets too brown, loosely tent the edges with some foil.
8. Let it cool before serving with fresh herbs or some green onion.

## *Cake Batter Chia Pudding with Coconut Whipped Cream*

*Serves:* 2-3

### Ingredients

- 6 Tbsp. Chia Seeds
- 1 C. Unsweetened Milk
- 6-8 Dates, Pitted And Chopped
- ¼ C. Almond Butter
- ¼ C. Rolled Oats
- 1 ½ Tbsp. Cacao Nibs
- 1 Tsp. Pure Vanilla Extract
- ¼ Tsp. Almond Extract
- 1 Can Full-Fat Coconut Milk, Chilled
- 2-4 Tsp. Pure Maple Syrup
- 1 Tsp. Pure Vanilla Extract

### Procedure

1. Stir the chia seeds with the milk in a bowl and add the almond butter, dates, and the oats. Cover and put them in the refrigerator for at least two hours, but overnight is preferred.
2. Scoop the mix into the blender with the nibs, half a teaspoon of vanilla, and a quarter of a teaspoon of the almond extract. Add the milk and blend until it's smooth and creamy. Add more milk if you need to but keep it as thick as possible.

3. Taste and add more vanilla if you desire and a few more drops of almond extract. Blend in more dates if it's not sweet enough. Refrigerate for a few hours.
4. As you chill the pudding, open the coconut milk and scrape off the solids. Avoid the liquid. Put the fat into a metal mixing bowl and beat it with two teaspoons of maple syrup and half a teaspoon of vanilla extract. Add more vanilla and maple if you desire. Beat until it's fluffy. Chill until you're ready to use it.
5. Serve the pudding with the whipped cream and a sprinkle of cacao nibs.

## *Banana Bread Breakfast Cookies*

*Serves:* 16

### Ingredients

- 2 Bananas, Mashed
- 2 C. Oats
- Optional Add-Ins:
  - Vanilla Beans
  - Vanilla Extract
  - Chocolate Chips
  - Butterscotch
  - Peanut Butter Chips
  - Dried Cranberries
  - Raisins
  - Coconut Flakes
  - Chopped Walnuts, Almond Or Pecans
  - Cocoa Nibs

### Procedure

1. Preheat your oven to 350 degrees Fahrenheit.
2. Put the oats into a blender or food processor and pulse until they look like flour.
3. Combine the banana and oats in a bowl and add in half a cup or a teaspoon of your optional additions.
4. Spray a baking sheet with some nonstick cooking spray and drop the dough onto the cookie sheet in tablespoons. Flatten with a spatula or the back of

the spoon and bake for twelve minutes or until the cookies are set. Remove and cool on a wire rack.

5.  They will keep for a few days covered or frozen for a few months.

## *Instant Avocado Toast*

(Serves: 1)

<u>Ingredients</u>

2 slices whole-wheat bread

1 cup avocado

freshly ground pepper

Himalayan salt

<u>Procedure</u>

1. Lightly toast the bread slices.

2. Mash the avocado meat and spread on the toasted bread.

3. Season with ground pepper and salt.

4. Serve.

# Quick Banana and Cinnamon Rolls

(Serves: 2)

### Ingredients

2 pcs. whole-wheat tortilla

¼ cup all-natural peanut butter

2 ripe bananas

cinnamon powder

### Procedure

1. Lay the tortilla on a plate and generously spread the peanut butter on the center.

2. Top with one ripe banana. Do the same procedure with the remaining tortilla wrap and banana.

3. Add a dash of cinnamon powder. Roll the tortilla.

4. Slice diagonally into half, or in bite-sized pieces. Serve.

# *Fruit and Nuts Oatmeal*

(Serves: 1)

Ingredients

¼ cup quick-cook oatmeal

2 tbsp. walnuts, chopped

½ cup strawberries, sliced

1 tsp. flax seed

½ cup low-fat milk

3 tbsp. honey

Procedure

1.  In a microwave oven-safe bowl, combine the oatmeal, milk and flax seed. Place in the microwave to cook for 2 minutes on high temperature.

2.  Top with strawberry slices, walnuts, and drizzle with honey.

3.  Serve.

# *Leafy Breakfast Skillet*

(Serves: 2)

## Ingredients

2 cups spinach, chopped

2 cups collard greens, chopped

1 cup mushrooms (your choice), sliced

2 organic eggs

½ onion, sliced thin

2 cloves of garlic, minced (divided into two)

1 tsp. dried oregano

1 tsp. chili flakes

1 tsp. cumin, ground

a pinch of sea salt

freshly ground pepper to taste

2 tbsp. Greek yogurt

1 tbsp. light coconut milk

1 tbsp. olive oil

cooking spray

## Procedure

1. Set oven at 400F.

2. Heat the olive oil in a pan over medium-high fire. Sauté the onion for about 3 minutes and allow it to caramelize. Throw in the chopped collard greens and season with salt and pepper. Cook for another 3 minutes and then add the ½ of the minced garlic, dried oregano, cumin, and chili flakes. Stir well.

3. Add the chopped spinach and then cook for 2 minutes or until the spinach has wilted. Remove from heat and set aside.

4. Coat a cast iron skillet with cooking spray. Transfer the cooked greens on the skillet leaving the liquid in the pot.

5. Place the sliced mushrooms on top of the cooked greens and create two wells where you will carefully crack the eggs.

6. Cook in the oven for about 8 to 10 minutes, or until the eggs are fully set.

7. While waiting for your eggs to cook, whisk together the coconut milk, the remainder of the minced garlic, and the Greek yogurt. When the eggs are cooked, use this sauce to drizzle over your cooked eggs, mushrooms, and greens.

8. Serve.

# *Spinach and Cheese Omelet*
(Serves: 1)

Ingredients

1 organic egg

2 tsp. olive oil (divided into 1 tsp. each)

1 cup baby spinach

1 tbsp. feta cheese, crumbled

pepper to taste

Sriracha sauce (optional)

Procedure

1.  Heat 1 tsp. olive oil on a nonstick pan over medium fire.

2.  Beat the egg in a bowl and then cook on the hot pan. Swirl the skillet from side to side to create an omelet and then cook for about a minute or 2 until the egg has set. Flip the egg and cook for another minute. Set aside.

3. Using the same pan, cook the spinach for about 1-2 minutes or until the spinach has wilted. Season with pepper.

4. Place the cooked egg on a plate and then top the half of the egg with the cooked spinach. Add the crumbled feta cheese on top. Fold the egg to create an omelet.

5. Serve with Sriracha sauce.

## *Egg and Cheese Breakfast Waffle*

(Serves: 2)

Ingredients

2 organic eggs

¼ cup parmesan cheese, grated

½ cup button mushrooms, chopped

¼ tsp. dried thyme

a dash of garlic powder

1 tbsp. olive oil

Procedure

1.  Combine all the ingredients in a bowl. Stir well.

2.  Heat your waffle iron and brush with the olive oil.

3.  Fill ½ to ¾ of your waffle iron with the mixture. Cook for about 4-5 minutes or until the waffle has set (this depends on the waffle iron you will use)

4.  Best served with avocadoes on the side.

## *Oatmeal Muffins on the Go*

(Serves: 12)

Ingredients

2 ½ old fashioned oats

2 ripe bananas, mashed

1 cup fresh raspberries

1 organic egg

¼ cup raw honey

1 tbsp. cinnamon powder

1 ½ tsp. baking powder

1 tbsp. coconut oil, melted

Procedure

1. Preheat oven to 350F.

2. Simply place all the ingredients in a large bowl and stir
   well.

3. Pour the batter on a greased muffin tray and place in the bake for 30 minutes, or until cooked.

4. Let it cool to room temperature before serving.

# *No-Cook Clean Eating Breakfast Bowl*
(Serves: 2)

Ingredients

1 cup old fashioned oats

1 cup soy milk, plain

1 cup raspberries or blueberries

4 tbsp. slivered almonds

Procedure

(This recipe must be prepared the night before.)

1.  Combine the oats with the soy milk and place in an air tight container to be stored in the fridge overnight.

2.  Before consuming, top with the berries and almonds.

# No-Guilt Pudding

(Serves: 2)

Ingredients

½ cup almond milk, vanilla flavor

1.2 cup Greek yogurt

3 tbsp. maple syrup (separate 1 tbsp.)

1 tsp. vanilla extract

4 tbsp. chia seeds

1 cup mixed berries

½ toasted almond, chopped

Procedure

(This recipe must be prepared the night before.)

1.  In a bowl combine the milk, yogurt, maple syrup, and vanilla extract. Stir carefully to mix all the ingredients.

2.  Then, slowly add the chia seeds by whisking it into the mixture. Cover the bowl with cling wrap and place in the fridge overnight.

3. The next morning, serve the pudding into two smaller bowls and then top with mixed berries and toasted almonds.

## *Mixed Berries and Cottage Cheese*

(Serves: 2)

<u>Ingredients</u>

1 cup low-fat cottage cheese

1 cup mixed berries (blueberries, strawberries, raspberries, etc.)

½ cup walnuts, chopped

2 tbsp. chia seeds

<u>Procedure</u>

1.  Mix all the ingredients except the chia seeds in two separate bowls.

2.  Sprinkle with chia seeds before serving.

# Chapter 4: Easy Whip Delicious and Healthy Meals

Have you always opted to order fast food because you don't have time to cook meals for yourself or your family? Well, that's about to change now! All you need is 15 minutes or less to cook clean eating recipes that the whole family will love.

## *Not Your Average Tuna Sandwich*

Prep time: 15 minutes

Ingredients:

1 5 oz. can of tuna chunks in water (drained)

2 slices of whole-wheat bread (toasted)

1 stalk green onion (finely chopped)

1 tbsp. low-fat mayo

½ tbsp. freshly squeezed lemon juice

4 tomato slices

¼ cup low-sodium cheddar (shredded)

salt and pepper to taste

Sriracha sauce (optional)

## Procedure

1. Preheat your broiler.

2. In a bowl, mix together the tuna chunks, green onion, mayo, lemon juice, salt, pepper, and Sriracha sauce.

3. Spread the tuna on top of each bread slices. Top with the tomato slices (2 on each read) and then followed by the shredded cheddar.

4. Place in the broiler and cook for about 4-5 minutes, or until the cheese melts.

5. Serve.

## *Classic Seared Salmon*

Prep time: 15 minutes

Ingredients:

10 oz. salmon fillet (about 2 pieces)

1 tsp. unsalted butter (divided into two ½ tsp.)

1 tsp. peppercorns

¼ cup freshly squeezed lemon juice

2 tsp. olive oil

salt

Procedure

1. Season the salmon with salt. Set aside.

2. Heat a skillet over medium fire. Grease the pan with olive oil and then place salmon fillets and cook for 5-6 minutes.

3. Turn off fire, but don't remove the salmon from the pan. Drizzle the fillets with lemon juice, top with butter, and season with salt and peppercorns.

4. Swirl the pan to make sure that the salmons are coated with the butter and peppercorns.

5. Serve with boiled potatoes, broccoli, and asparagus on the side.

# Steak and Potatoes Plate

Prep time: 15 minutes

Ingredients:

½ kg. sirloin steak (about 2 pcs)

¼ kg. baby potatoes

½ tbsp. white miso

½ tbsp. rice wine vinegar

½ tsp. honey

½ tsp. ginger (minced)

¼ sesame oil

2 tbsps. olive oil (divided into 2)

salt and pepper

2 pcs. green onions (sliced thin)

Procedure

1.  Using a fork or a small knife, pierce the baby potatoes. Place them in a microwave oven-safe bowl, and cover loosely with a plastic wrap. Cook on high for 5 minutes, or until the potatoes are tender. Set aside.

2.  Season the steak with salt and pepper. While waiting for the potatoes to cook, heat 1 tbsp. of olive oil in a skillet over medium fire. Place the steak and cook for 3 minutes each side. Set aside.

3. While cooking the steak, place the white miso, rice wine vinegar, honey, ginger, sesame oil, and the remaining olive oil in a small bowl and whisk thoroughly.

4. Cut the steak into ¼ inch thick strips and place on a plate with the potatoes. Drizzle with the vinegar and oil dressing. Garnish with green onions.

# Bow Tie Pasta and Veggie Salad

Prep time: 12-15 minutes

Ingredients:

250g whole-wheat bow tie pasta

2 cloves of garlic (minced)

½ tbsp. fresh basil (chopped)

½ tsp. fresh thyme

½ tbsp. parsley (chopped)

½ tbsp. capers (drained)

1-cup arugula (chopped)

1-cup cherry tomatoes (sliced in half)

1-cup broccoli (chopped)

¼ tsp. chili flakes

¼ tsp. black pepper

salt to taste

¼ cup olive oil

grated Parmesan cheese

Procedure

1. Cook the pasta according to the packaging (usually takes 9-10 minutes).

2. Blanch the broccoli in hot water and set aside.

3.  While waiting for the pasta to cook, heat olive oil in a skillet over medium fire. Sauté the garlic for a minute. Add the capers, chili flakes, and black pepper and sauté for another minute.

4.  Add the cooked pasta (drained) to the pan along with the chopped arugula and cook for 1-2 minutes or until the arugula has wilted. Add the remaining herbs and mix well.

5.  Turn of the heat and add the cherry tomatoes. Toss carefully to incorporate all the ingredients.

6.  Serve with grated Parmesan on top.

# Refreshing Salad

Prep time: 5-8 minutes

Ingredients:

2 cucumbers (sliced thin)

2 cups cherry tomatoes (cut in half)

1 small onion (sliced thin)

1 tbsp. extra virgin olive oil

2 tbsp. balsamic vinegar

1 tsp. Dijon mustard

1 tsp. maple syrup

salt and pepper

Procedure

1. In a medium-sized bowl, whisk the olive oil, vinegar, mustard, maple syrup, salt, and pepper. Combine well.

2. Throw in the cucumbers, tomatoes, and onion slices and toss until the vegetables are well coated with the dressing.

3. Serve.

# *Shrimp in Angel Hair Pasta*

Prep time: 10 minutes

Ingredients:

250g angel hair pasta (preferably whole-wheat)

½ lb. deveined shrimp (peeled)

1 tbsp. olives (chopped)

1 tbsp. flat leaf parsley (chopped)

1 clove of garlic (minced)

1-cup spinach (chopped)

½ cup cherry tomatoes (cut in half)

¼ cup low-sodium chicken stock.

1/8 cup white whine

½ tbsp. olive oil

Procedure

1. Cook the pasta according to the packaging. (About 8-10 minutes)

2. While waiting for the pasta to cook, heat the oil in a pan over medium-high fire. Add the shrimps, season with salt, and cook for 4-5 minutes. Place the shrimp on a plate. Set aside.

3.  Using the same pan, cook the garlic, parsley and olives for 1 minute. Add the baby spinach, tomatoes, chicken broth, and wine. Cover the pan and let it simmer for 3 minutes. Turn off the heat.

4.  Add the shrimp and pasta to the pan and stir.

5.  Serve.

## *Broiled Asian Salmon*

Prep time: 10 minutes

<u>Ingredients:</u>

5 oz. salmon fillet

½ low-sodium soy sauce

½ tbsp. honey

salt and pepper

cooked brown rice

<u>Procedure</u>

1. Preheat your broiler.

2. Whisk the soy sauce and honey in a small bowl. Set aside.

3. Season the fillets with salt and pepper, and place in the broiler to cook for 5 minutes.

4. Remove from the broiler and drizzle with the soy and honey sauce. Place back in the broiler to cook for another 3-5 minutes.

5. Serve with brown rice.

# Quinoa Salad with Asparagus, Dates, and Orange

*Serves:* 8

## Ingredients

- 1 Tsp. Olive Oil

- ½ C. Minced White Onion

- 1 C. Uncooked Quinoa

- 2 C. Water

- ½ Tsp. Kosher Salt

- 1 C. Fresh Orange Sections

- ¼ C. Chopped Pecans, Toasted

- 2 Tbsp. Minced Red Onion

- 5 Dates, Pitted And Chopped

- ½ Lb. Sliced Asparagus, Steamed And Chilled

- ½ Jalapeño Pepper, Chopped

- 2 Tbsp. Fresh Lemon Juice

- 1 Tbsp. Extra Virgin Olive Oil

- ¼ Tsp. Kosher Salt

- ¼ Tsp. Freshly Ground Black Pepper

- 1 Garlic Clove, Minced

- 2 Tbsp. Chopped Fresh Mint

- Mint Sprigs

Procedure

1.  To prepare your salad, heat a teaspoon of oil in a nonstick skillet over medium heat. Sauté the onion for two minutes. Add the quinoa and sauté another five minutes. Add two cups of water and half a teaspoon of salt. Bring that to a boil. Cover and reduce the heat to a simmer for fifteen minutes. Remove it from the heat and allow it to stand for fifteen minutes or until the water has been absorbed. Transfer the quinoa to a bowl and add the orange, along with the following five ingredients. Toss to combine.

2.  Combine the juice with the following four ingredients in a bowl and stir with a whisk. Pour the dressing over the salad and toss to coat. Sprinkle with the chopped mint and garnish with a sprig of mint if you desire. Serve at room temperature.

# Fennel and Spinach Salad with Shrimp and Balsamic Vinaigrette

*Serves:* 4

## Ingredients

- 3 Slices Bacon

- 1 Lb. Jumbo Shrimp, Peeled And Deveined

- 2 C. Sliced Fennel Bulb

- 1 C. Grape Tomatoes, Halved

- ½ C. Sliced Red Onion

- 9 Oz. Fresh Baby Spinach

- 2 Tbsp. Minced Shallots

- 3 Tbsp. Extra-Virgin Olive Oil

- 1 Tbsp. Balsamic Vinegar

- 1 Tsp. Dijon Mustard

- ¼ Tsp. Black Pepper

- ¼ Tsp. Salt

## Procedure

1. Cook the bacon in a skillet over medium heat until it's crisp. Remove it from the pan and reserve the drippings. Crumble the bacon. Add the shrimp to the pan and cook it for two minutes.

2. Combine the bacon with two cups of fennel, tomatoes, onion, and spinach in a bowl. Combine the rest of the ingredients in a bowl and stir with a whisk. Add the

shrimp and the dressing to the salad mix and toss to combine.

# Oven-Fried Sweet Potatoes

*Serves:* 7

## Ingredients

- 4 Sweet Potatoes, Peeled And Sliced

- 1 Tbsp. Olive Oil

- ¼ Tsp. Salt

- ¼ Tsp. Pepper

- Vegetable Cooking Spray

- 1 Tbsp. Minced Fresh Parsley

- 1 Tsp. Grated Orange Rind

- 1 Small Garlic Clove, Minced

## Procedure

1. Combine the first four ingredients and toss them in a bowl. Arrange the potato slices in a single layer on a greased baking sheet. Bake at 400 degrees Fahrenheit for half an hour or until they're tender. Turn them after fifteen minutes.

2. Combine the orange rind, parsley, and garlic in a bowl. Stir it well and sprinkle it over the sweet potato slices before serving.

# Crab Salad-Stuffed Eggs

*Serves:* 8

## Ingredients

- 2 C. Sliced Radishes
- 1 Tbsp. Fresh Lemon Juice, Divided
- ½ Tsp. Salt, Divided
- 8 Eggs
- ¼ Tsp. Black Pepper
- 2 Tbsp. Extra-Virgin Olive Oil
- 3 Tbsp. Plain Greek-Style Fat-Free Yogurt
- 1 C. Lump Crabmeat, Drained
- ¼ C. Minced Celery
- 1 Tsp. Dry Mustard
- 24 Butter Lettuce Leaves

## Procedure

1. Combine the radishes with two teaspoons of lemon juice and a quarter of a teaspoon of salt in a bowl. Cover and chill for half an hour.

2. Put the eggs in a pan and cover with cold water to an inch above them. Bring them to a boil and reduce the heat. Simmer them for ten minutes. Put them in ice

water and cool them completely. Gently crack them and peel them under cold water.

3.  Cut them in half lengthwise and remove the yolks. Press the yolks through a sieve and set aside a tablespoon. Combine the rest of the lemon juice with the yolks, a quarter teaspoon of salt, and the pepper in a bowl. Add the oil slowly and whisk as you add the oil. Stir in the yogurt. Add the crab, mustard, and celery and stir until it's combined. Taste the filling and adjust your seasonings if necessary.

4.  Arrange three lettuce leaves on eight plates and cut a thin slice from the bottom of the egg white. Pile the crab into the egg white halves and put two on each plate on one side of the lettuce. Sprinkle them with the yolk over the egg white halves. Arrange a quarter of a cup of the radish mix on the other side of the servings.

## *Arugula, Grape, and Sunflower Seed Salad*

*Serves:* 6

Ingredients

- 1 Tsp. Honey

- 3 Tbsp. Red Wine Vinegar

- ½ Tsp. Stone-Ground Mustard

- 1 Tsp. Maple Syrup

- 2 Tsp. Grapeseed Oil

- 2 C. Red Grapes, Halved

- 7 C. Baby Arugula

- 1 Tsp. Thyme, Chopped

- 2 Tbsp. Sunflower Seed Kernels, Toasted

- ¼ Tsp. Salt

- ¼ Tsp. Black Pepper

Procedure

1. Combine the honey, vinegar, syrup, and mustard in a bowl. Add the oil slowly and stir with a whisk.

2. Combine the remaining ingredients in a bowl, drizzle with the vinegar mix, and sprinkle with some salt and pepper. Toss to coat.

# Carrot Soup with Yogurt

*Serves:* 8

## Ingredients

- 2 Tsp. Dark Sesame Oil

- ⅓ C. Sliced Shallots

- 1 Lb. Baby Carrots, Peeled And Sliced

- 2 C. Chicken Broth

- 1 Tsp. Grated Peeled Fresh Ginger

- ½ C. 2% Greek-Style Plain Yogurt

- 8 Fresh Mint Sprigs

## Procedure

1. Heat the oil in a pan over medium heat and sauté the shallots until they're tender. Add the carrots and cook for another four minutes. Add the broth and bring it to a boil. Cover and reduce the heat to a simmer for twenty-five minutes. Add the ginger and cook another eight minutes. Cover and allow it to rest at room temperature for five minutes.

2. Pour half the mix into a blender and remove the center piece of the blender lid. Secure the lid on the blender. Put a clean towel over the blender lid to avoid splattering and blend until it's smooth. Pour it into a bowl and repeat with the rest of the mixture. Return the soup to the pan and heat it over medium heat for two minutes.

3. Spoon it into bowls and top with the yogurt and the mint sprigs.

# Nutty Warm Brussels Sprouts Salad

*Serves:* 6

## Ingredients

- 1 ½ Tsp. Extra-Virgin Olive Oil, Divided

- 1 Garlic Clove, Minced

- ⅓ C. Breadcrumbs

- ¾ Lb. Brussels Sprouts, Halved

- ¼ Tsp. Salt

- ⅛ Tsp. Freshly Ground Black Pepper

- 1 ½ Tbsp. Minced Walnuts, Toasted

- ½ Oz. Shaved Asiago Cheese

## Procedure

1. Heat a teaspoon of oil in a skillet over medium heat and sauté the garlic for a minute. Add the breadcrumbs and cook another minute. Transfer the garlic mix to a small bowl.

2. Separate the leaves from the sprouts and quarter the cores. Heat the rest of the oil over medium heat and add the leaves and cores to the pan. Sauté for eight minutes or until the leaves have wilted and the cores are tender. Remove it from the heat and toss with the breadcrumb mix, salt and pepper. Top with the cheese and walnuts.

# Seared Tuna Niçoise

*Serves:* 4

## Ingredients

- 3 Eggs
- 1 ½ C. Small Red Potatoes, Quartered
- 1 C. Haricots Verts, Trimmed
- 2 6 Oz. Tuna Steaks
- ½ Tsp. Kosher Salt, Divided
- ¼ Tsp. Black Pepper
- 2 Tbsp. Extra-Virgin Olive Oil
- 3 Tbsp. Red Wine Vinegar
- 1 Tsp. Dijon Mustard
- ⅔ C. Grape Tomatoes, Halved
- ¼ C. Pitted And Quartered Niçoise Olives

## Procedure

1. Put the eggs in a pot and cover them with water to an inch above the eggs. Bring them to a boil and remove them from the heat. Let them rest fifteen minutes before you drain them, cool them in ice water for five minutes, and peel them. Quarter the eggs.

2. Put the potatoes in the pan and cover them with water. Bring them to a boil and reduce the heat to a simmer for twelve minutes. Add the beans and cook them for three minutes. Drain and plunge the beans into some ice water for a minute. Drain them well.

3. Heat a skillet over medium heat and coat the pan with cooking spray. Sprinkle the tuna with a quarter of a teaspoon of salt and pepper each. Add the tuna to the pan and cook for two minutes on either side or until it's reached your desired degree of doneness. Cut it thinly across the grain.

4. Combine the rest of the salt, oil, mustard and vinegar in a bowl and stir with a whisk. Add the tomatoes and olives, toss them. Divide the eggs, beans, potatoes, and tuna amongst four plates and top with the tomato mixture.

# *Minty Millet & Pomegranate Salad*

*Serves:* 4

## Ingredients

- 2 C. Cooked Millet
- 1 Bulb Fennel, Sliced
- 1 C. Chickpeas, Drained & Rinsed
- ¼ C. Or So, Sliced Red Cabbage
- ¼ C. Scallions Chopped Scallions
- ⅓ C. Pomegranate Seeds
- ⅓ C. Toasted Pistachios
- 4 C. Baby Salad Greens
- 1 C. Mint Leaves
- 2 Tbsp. Olive Oil
- 2 Tbsp. Tahini
- 3 Tbsp. Fresh Squeezed Lemon
- 3 Tbsp. Fresh Squeezed Orange
- 2 Tsp. Maple Syrup
- Salt And Pepper

## Procedure

1. Whisk the olive oil through the salt and pepper together and set it aside.

2. Toss the chickpeas into a skillet with some olive oil and a little salt and pepper until they're browned.

3. Toss the salad ingredients with the dressing and taste to adjust the seasonings. Serve.

# *Shrimp and Avocado Summer Rolls*

*Serves:* 6

## Ingredients

- 9 Shrimp, Boiled, Peeled And Halved Lengthwise
- Boston Lettuce, Torn
- 2 Carrots, Sliced
- 1 Seedless Cucumber, Sliced
- 1 C. Red Cabbage, Shredded
- 1 Avocado, Sliced
- About 1 Oz. Cellophane Noodles, Optional
- 1 Tbsp. Seasoned Rice Vinegar
- Fresh Cilantro
- Fresh Basil
- Spring Roll Wrappers, Round

## Procedure

1. Cover the noodles with boiling water and allow them to stand for ten minutes.
2. Drain and toss them with the vinegar.
3. In a pie plate, add enough hot water to come halfway up the side.
4. Submerge the spring roll wrapper in the water for half a minute or until it's soft and pliable.
5. Lay the wrapper on some parchment paper.

6. Put three shrimp halves with the cut side up in the middle of the bottom half of your wrapper.

7. Arrange the other ingredients with the shrimp and leave an inch on the sides.

8. Bring the bottom of your wrapper up and over the ingredient and roll it gently, tucking in the sides as you go.

9. Set it aside until they're all assembled. Cut in half and serve with some dipping sauce.

# Chapter 5 – Dinner for Motivation

Dinner is the time of day where everyone is supposed to sit down around the table and enjoy a healthy, comforting meal. Anymore, dinner is usually filled with heavily processed, frozen foods that are unhealthy and destroy your motivation for the next day. Set yourself up right with a healthy dinner.

## *Chicken with Brussels Sprouts and Mustard Sauce*

*Serves:* 4

### Ingredients

- 2 Tbsp. Olive Oil, Divided

- 4 Skinless, Boneless Chicken Breast Halves

- ½ Tsp. Salt, Divided

- ¼ Tsp. Pepper

- ¾ C. Chicken Broth, Divided

- ¼ C. Apple Cider

- 2 Tbsp. Whole-Grain Dijon Mustard

- 2 Tbsp. Butter, Divided

- 1 Tbsp. Flat-Leaf Parsley, Chopped

- 12 Oz. Brussels Sprouts, Trimmed And Halved

## Procedure

1. Preheat your oven to 450 degrees Fahrenheit.

2. Heat an ovenproof skillet over high heat and add a tablespoon of oil. Sprinkle the chicken with a quarter of a teaspoon of salt and pepper and add it to the pan. Cook it for three minutes or until it's browned. Turn the chicken and put it in the oven. Bake for nine minutes or until it's done. Remove it from the pan and keep it warm.

3. Heat the pan over medium-high heat and add half a cup of broth and the cider. Bring it to a boil and scrape the bottom to loosen the browned bits. Reduce the heat to a simmer for four minutes or until it's thickened. Whisk in the mustard with a tablespoon of butter and parsley.

4. Heat the rest of the oil and a tablespoon of butter in a skillet over medium heat. Add the sprouts and sauté for two minutes. Add the rest of the salt and a quarter of a cup of broth to the pan. Cover and cook for four minutes or until it's tender. Serve the sprouts with the chicken and the sauce.

# Lemony Chicken Kebabs with Tomato Parsley Salad

*Serves:* 4

## Ingredients

- 3 Tbsp. Lemon Juice, Divided
- 1 Tbsp. Minced Garlic, Divided
- 1 ½ Tsp. Dried Oregano, Divided
- ¾ Tsp. Kosher Salt, Divided
- ¾ Tsp. Black Pepper, Divided
- 3 Tbsp. Extra-Virgin Olive Oil, Divided
- 4 Skinless, Boneless Chicken Breast Halves, Cubed
- 2 C. Fresh Parsley Leaves
- 1 C. Chopped Cherry Tomatoes

## Procedure

1. Combine two tablespoons of lemon juice with two teaspoons of garlic, a teaspoon of oregano, half a teaspoon of salt, and half a teaspoon of pepper in a bowl. Add a tablespoon of the oil and stir it with a whisk. Add the chicken and stir. Marinate in the refrigerator for two hours.

2. Remove the chicken and discard the marinade. Thread the chicken onto skewers and heat a grill pan over high heat. Add the skewers and cook t hem for six minutes, turning them often, until they're done.

3. Combine one tablespoon of lemon juice with a teaspoon of garlic, a half a teaspoon of oregano, a quarter of a

teaspoon of salt, and a quarter of a teaspoon of pepper in a bowl. Add the two tablespoons of olive oil and stir with a whisk. Add the parsley and tomatoes and toss them to coat. Serve the chicken over the salad.

# *Tenderloin Steaks with Red Onion Marmalade*

*Serves:* 4

## Ingredients

- Cooking Spray
- 1 Red Onion, Sliced
- 2 Tbsp. Red Wine Vinegar
- ½ Tsp. Salt, Divided
- ¼ Tsp. Black Pepper
- 2 Tbsp. Honey
- 1 Tsp. Dried Thyme
- 4 Beef Tenderloin Steaks, Trimmed

## Procedure

1. Preheat your broiler.

2. Heat a skillet over medium heat and coat the pan with some cooking spray. Add the onion to the pan and cover. Cook it for three minutes. Add the honey, vinegar, and a quarter of a teaspoon of salt to the pan. Reduce the heat and simmer for eight minutes until it's thick, stirring occasionally.

3. Sprinkle a quarter of a teaspoon of salt, thyme, and pepper over the beef. Put the beef on a broiler pan that's been greased and broil for four minutes on either side or until it reaches our desired degree of doneness. Serve with the onion mixture.

# Peppercorn Crusted Beef Tenderloin with Gremolata

*Serve:* 4

## Ingredients

- 4 Beef Tenderloin Steaks, Trimmed

- Cooking Spray

- 2 Tsp. Cracked Black Pepper

- ½ Tsp. Salt, Divided

- 4 Tsp. Canola Oil, Divided

- ¼ C. Flat-Leaf Parsley, Chopped

- 3 Tbsp. Chopped Fresh Cilantro

- 1 ½ Tsp. Garlic, Chopped

- 1 Tsp. Chopped Fresh Oregano

- ½ Tsp. Grated Lemon Rind

- 1 Tbsp. Fresh Lemon Juice

- ¼ Tsp. Crushed Red Pepper

## Procedure

1. Coat the steak with the cooking spray and sprinkle with the pepper and a quarter of a teaspoon of salt. Heat a skillet over medium heat and add a teaspoon of oil. Swirl

it to coat the pan. Add the steaks to the pan and cook for three minutes on either side.

2.  Combine the rest of the oil, salt, parsley, and the remaining ingredients in a bowl. Stir with a whisk. Serve over the steak.

# *Arctic Char with Orange-Caper Relish*

*Serves:* 4

## Ingredients

- 1 C. Orange Sections
- 2 Tbsp. Red Onion, Sliced
- 1 Tbsp. Fresh Flat-Leaf Parsley, Chopped
- 1 Tbsp. Capers, Minced
- 1 Tsp. Grated Orange Rind
- 1 Tbsp. Fresh Orange Juice
- 1 Tbsp. Extra-Virgin Olive Oil
- 1 Tsp. Rice Vinegar
- ⅛ Tsp. Ground Red Pepper
- 4 Arctic Char Fillets
- ½ Tsp. Kosher Salt
- ½ Tsp. Freshly Ground Black Pepper
- Cooking Spray

## Procedure

1. Combine the first nine ingredients in a bowl and toss them to combine. Cover and chill until you're ready to serve.

2.  Heat a skillet over high heat and season the fish with salt and pepper. Coat the pan with some cooking spray and sear the fish on either side for four minutes. Put one fillet on a plate and top with a quarter of a cup of the relish.

# *Grilled Pork Chops with Two-Melon Salsa*

*Serves:* 4

Ingredients

- 1 C. Seedless Watermelon, Chopped
- 1 C. Honeydew Melon, Chopped
- 3 Tbsp. Minced Sweet Onion
- 1 Tbsp. Minced Jalapeño Pepper
- 1 Tbsp. Fresh Cilantro, Chopped
- 1 Tbsp. Fresh Lime Juice
- ⅛ Tsp. Salt
- 2 Tsp. Canola Oil
- 1 ½ Tsp. Chili Powder
- ½ Tsp. Garlic Powder
- ½ Tsp. Salt
- ¼ Tsp. Black Pepper
- 4 Pork Chops, Trimmed

Procedure

1. To make the salsa, combine the first seven ingredients and set them aside.

2.  To prepare the chops, heat a grill pan over high heat. Combine the oil and the following four ingredients in a bowl. Rub the oil mix over the chops and coat the pan with some cooking spray or oil. Add the pork to the pan and cook for four minutes on either side. Serve with the salsa.

# *Tuna Scaloppini with Onion, Mint, and Almond Topping*

*Serves:* 4

## Ingredients

- ¼ C. Minced Almonds

- ¼ C. Fresh Tangerine Juice

- 2 Tbsp. Minced Red Onion

- 2 Tbsp. Minced Fresh Mint

- 1 Tbsp. Extra-Virgin Olive Oil

- ½ Tsp. Minced Fennel Seeds

- ½ Tsp. Fine Sea Salt, Divided

- ½ Tsp. Freshly Ground Black Pepper, Divided

- 4 Yellowfin Tuna Steaks, Sliced In Half Horizontally

- Cooking Spray

## Procedure

1. Combine the first six ingredients in a bowl and stir in a quarter of a teaspoon of salt and pepper.

2. Sprinkle the fish with the rest of the salt and pepper. Heat a skillet over high heat and coat the pan with some oil. Add the fish and cook for one minute on either side. Repeat with the rest of the fish. Serve with the almond mix.

# Avocado and Quinoa Stuffed Acorn Squash

*Serves:* 6-8

## Ingredients

- 4 Small Acorn Squash, Sliced In Half
- 2 Tbsp. Olive Oil
- 1 Medium Onion
- 3 Cloves Of Garlic, Minced
- 1 Tsp. Cumin
- 1 Tsp. Coriander
- 1 4-Oz. Can Of Green Chiles
- 1 ½ C. Cooked Quinoa
- 1 Can Black Beans, Drained And Rinsed
- ¼ C. Chopped Scallions
- ¼ C. Toasted Pepitas
- ¼ C. Feta Cheese, Optional
- 2 Avocados, Chopped
- A Few Squeezes Of Lime
- Salt & Pepper

## Procedure

1. Preheat your oven to 400 degrees Fahrenheit.

2.   Cut the squash in half and scoop out the seeds. Drizzle it with oil and season it with salt and pepper.

3.   Roast it with the cut side up for fifty minutes or until the squash is tender in the middle and browned along the edges.

4.   In the meantime, heat the oil in a skillet over medium heat and sauté the onion with a few pinches of salt and pepper. Cook until it's translucent and then add the cumin, garlic, and coriander. Stir and add the chilies. Stir again and then add the beans, quinoa, scallions, feta, pepitas, and a little lime juice. Season with salt and pepper to taste.

5.   Remove the skillet from the heat to allow the mix to cool and stir in the chopped avocado. Season again.

6.   Scoop the filling into the squash and serve.

# Cauliflower Risotto

*Serves:* 2

## Ingredients

- ½ Cauliflower, Processed To Make Rice
- 2 C. Fresh Spinach, Chopped
- 1 Can White Beans, Divided And Drained
- ½ C. Vegetable Broth
- 1 Shallot, Chopped
- 3 Cloves Garlic, Minced
- 2 Tbsp. Sundried Tomatoes, Packed In Oil And Drained
- 1 Tbsp. Capers
- ½ Tsp. Fresh Thyme
- Toasted Pine Nuts

## Procedure

1. In a pot, heat a tablespoon of oil over medium heat. Sauté the shallots, thyme, and garlic for two to three minutes or until they're fragrant.

2. Put half the can of beans and the vegetable broth in the pot and simmer for five minutes.

3. Blend the contents with an immersion blender until it's creamy and smooth.

4. Add the cauliflower, tomatoes, the rest of the beans, and the spinach. Cover and allow it to heat up for five minutes.

5. Add the capers before serving and garnish with the pine nuts.

# Harissa Chicken Stuffed Eggplant

*Serves:* 2

## Ingredients

- 1 Eggplant
- 2 Tbsp. Extra Virgin Olive Oil, Separated
- ¾ Lb. Chicken Breast, Cubed
- 1 C. Mushrooms, Chopped
- 1 Onion, Chopped
- 2 Garlic Cloves, Crushed
- 2 C. Spinach
- 1 Can Tomatoes, Chopped
- 2 Tbsp. Mina Harissa Sauce
- 1 Tbsp. Basil
- 1 Tsp. Garlic Powder
- Salt
- Red Pepper Flakes

## Procedure

1. Preheat your oven to 375 degrees Fahrenheit.

2. Slice eggplant in half and scoop the center out. Set it aside.

3. Brush the eggplant with the oil and put it on a lined baking sheet. Bake for fifteen minutes or until it's soft.

4. In a skillet, heat the other tablespoon of oil and sauté the garlic.

5. Add the onion, mushrooms, chicken, and the rest of the eggplant.

6. Cook until the chicken is done.

7. Add in the mina, tomatoes, and spices.

8. Add in the spinach and mix until it's sautéed.

9. Taste and adjust the spices as you desire.

10. Put the mix into eggplant bowls and bake for ten minutes.

# Grilled Chicken on Zucchini Noodles

(Serves: 2-3)

## Ingredients

24 oz. chicken breast, skin removed

2 large zucchini

½ tsp. cumin

1 juice of lime

¾ cup fresh basil, finely chopped

Salt and pepper to taste

1 tbsp. olive oil

## Procedure

1. To make the noodles, simply use a mandolin to create noodle-like strips of the zucchini. Set aside.

2. Season the chicken with salt, pepper, and cumin, and cook on the grill on medium-high temperature until done. Slice and transfer on a plate and set aside.

3. Drizzle the oil in a pan over high heat. Throw in the zucchini noodles and cook for about 1-2 minutes. Add the basil, season again with salt, and cook for 2-3 minutes. Turn off the heat then drizzle with lime juice. Stir carefully.

4. Add the chicken slices on top of the noodles. Serve.

*Wild Rice Fry on Baked Zucchini*

(Serves: 2-3)

<u>Ingredients</u>

2-3 cups cooked wild rice

2 pcs. zucchini, cut length wise

1 red onion, chopped

2 cloves of garlic, minced

1 large tomato, chopped

1 medium-sized bell pepper, chopped

2 tbsp. pine nuts

2 tbsp. dill, chopped

2 tbsp. parsley, chopped

2 tbsp. fresh mint, hopped

¼ tsp. paprika

salt and pepper to taste

2 tbsp. extra virgin olive oil

2 tbsp. freshly squeezed lime juice

<u>Procedure</u>

1. Set oven at 400F.

2. Using a teaspoon, scoop the insides of the zucchini, to create room for the stir-fried wild rice.

3.  Heat the olive oil in a pan over medium high fire.

4.  Toss the pine nuts and roast them for 2-3 minutes.

5.  Add the onions and sauté for 2 minutes or until the onions turn translucent. Add the minced garlic, tomato, bell pepper, and season with the paprika, salt, and pepper and cook for 2 minutes.

6.  Add the cooked rice to the pan and let it marry with the ingredients for about a minute. Turn off the fire and then add the dill, parsley, and fresh mint. Mix well. Set aside.

7.  Place the zucchini on a baking sheet coated with olive oil and fill them with the wild rice. Place in the oven to bake for 40 minutes.

8.  Drizzle with lime juice on top before serving.

# Quinoa and Berries Salad

(Serves: 2)

## Ingredients

½ cup quinoa

1 cup arugula

1 cup alfalfa sprouts

½ cup strawberries, cut in half

½ cup blueberries

1 cup ripe mango, chopped

1 tbsp. mint leaves, chopped

½ cup walnuts

¼ cup slivered almonds

**For the dressing:**

2 tbsp. extra virgin olive oil

4 tbsp. lime juice

1 tsp. honey

1 tsp. chia seeds

Salt and pepper to taste

## Procedure

1. Cook the quinoa according to the package instructions.

2. While waiting for the quinoa to cook, whisk all the dressing ingredients in a small bowl, set aside.

3. Place the cooked quinoa on a salad bowl and toss along with the remaining ingredients.

4. Pour the prepared dressing over the quinoa and berries and toss until all the ingredients marry.

5. Allow to sit in the fridge for about 30 minutes before serving.

## *Shrimp and Spinach Salad*

(Serves: 2-3)

Ingredients

16 oz. shrimp, peeled and vein removed

4 cups baby spinach

1 bulb fennel, sliced thin

1 cup cherry tomatoes, cut in half

1 small red onion, sliced thin

2 tbsp. shallots, finely chopped

1 tbsp. olive oil

**For dressing:**

1 tbsp. balsamic vinegar

3 tbsp. extra virgin olive oil

1 tsp. mustard

salt and pepper to taste

Procedure

1. Heat the oil on a pan over medium fire. Add the shrimp to the hot pan and cook for 2 minutes.

2. In a salad bowl, toss together the baby spinach, fennel, tomatoes, onion, and shallots.

3. Whisk all the dressing ingredients together in a small bowl and pour over the salad.

4. Add the cooked shrimp to the salad bowl and toss well.

5. Serve.

## *Zesty Chicken Bake*

(Serves: 2)

Ingredients

2 pcs chicken breast, bone and skin removed

½ cup low-sodium chicken stock (divided into ¼)

2 cups Brussel sprouts, cut into two

½ tbsp. parsley, chopped

4 tbsp. apple cider

1 tbsp. Dijon mustard

1 tbsp. ghee or butter (divided into ½)

1 tbsp. olive oil (divided into ½)

salt and pepper to taste

Procedure

1. Set oven at 450F.

2. Using an ovenproof pan, heat ½ tbsp. olive oil on high temperature. Season the chicken with salt and pepper and cook on the pan for 3 minutes.

3. Then place the pan in the oven with the chicken o cook for 10 minutes. When done, remove chicken from the pan and set aside.

4. Using the same pan, heat the ¼ cup chicken stock with the apple cider on medium-high heat. Bring to a boil. When the stock is boiling, reduce the heat to medium-

low and let it simmer until it turns thick, or for about 4-5 minutes.

5. Stir in the mustard, ghee, and chopped parsley. Set aside

6. In a separate pan, heat the remaining ½ tbsp. oil on a nonstick pan over medium-high fire. Sauté the Brussels sprout halves for 2 minutes. Pour over the other half of the chicken stock and season with salt. Cover and let it cook for 4-5 minutes.

7. Serve the baked chicken with the sauce and crispy Brussels sprouts on the side.

# 5-Ingredient Grilled Chicken

(Serves: 2)

## Ingredients

2 chicken breast, bone and skin removed

1 small bell pepper, cut into half and seeds removed

1 tbsp. olives, chopped

½ tbsp. basil, chopped

3 tbsp. feta cheese, crumbled

salt and pepper

## Procedure

1. Pre-heat your broiler.

2. Lay the bell pepper on a baking sheet with aluminum foil and place in the broiler to cook for 15 minutes.

3. When done cooking, place the bell peppers inside a Ziploc bag and let it sit, sealed, for another 15 minutes. When done, remove the skin and then chop finely.

4. Pre-heat the grill to medium-high temperature.

5. In a bowl, mix the chopped bell pepper, olives, basil, and feta cheese. Using a sharp knife, cut a slit horizontally on the thickest part of the chicken breast to form a pocket.

6. Generously stuff the bell pepper mixture into the pocket and close it using a toothpick.

7. Season the chicken with salt and pepper and place on the grill to cook for 6 minutes on each side.

8. When cooked, placed the chicken on a serving plate and cover with foil. Set aside for 10 minutes before serving.

# Broiled Steak Sirloin

(Serves: 2)

Ingredients

2 4 oz. sirloin steak, trimmed

1 cup red onion, cut into rings

1 tbsp. raw honey

1 tbsp. red wine vinegar

½ tsp. thyme

salt and pepper to taste

1 tbsp. olive oil

Procedure

1. Pre-heat your broiler.

2. Heat the oil on a non-stick skillet over medium-high fire. When the oil is hot, place the onions in the pan, and cover for 3 minutes.

3. Reduce the heat and pour the red wine vinegar and honey with the onions. Allow to simmer for 8 minutes, uncovered. Stir occasionally.

4. Meanwhile, season the steaks with salt, pepper and dried thyme on both sides. Place the beef on a pan coated with oil or cooking spray and cook in the broiler for 4 minutes on each side.

5. Serve the steak long with the onion sauce.

# Seared Tuna and Veggies

(Serves: 2)

## Ingredients

1 6 oz. tuna steak

1 cup baby potatoes

½ cherry tomatoes, cut in half

1 bunch string beans

½ tsp. Dijon mustard

2 tbsp. extra virgin olive oil

1 ½ red wine vinegar

Salt and pepper to taste

## Procedure

1. Place the baby potatoes in a small pot with water and bring into a boil. Reduce the temperature and allow to simmer for 12 minutes. Before turning off the fire, add the string beans to the pot and cook for 3 minutes.

2. Remove the beans from the pot and soak in ice cold water for a minute.

3. Season the tuna with salt and pepper.

4. Heat cast iron skillet coated with cooking spray on medium-high fire and cook the tuna for about 2 minutes on each side. When done, thinly slice the tuna across and place on two separate plates.

5. In a small bowl, whisk the mustard, olive oil and red wine vinegar. Throw in the cherry tomatoes and toss carefully.

6. Serve the seared tuna with the tomatoes on top with the baby tomatoes and string beans on the side.

# Grilled Chops with Refreshing Salsa

(Serves: 2)

<u>Ingredients</u>

2 4oz. boneless pork chops, trimmed

¼ tsp. garlic powder

¾ tsp. chili flakes

1 tsp. olive oil

Salt and pepper to taste

**For the salsa:**

1 cup watermelon, chopped and seeds removed

½ tbsp. jalapeno, seeds removed and finely chopped

½ tbsp. cilantro, chopped

2 tbsp. sweet onion, finely chopped

½ tbsp. freshly squeezed lime juice

a pinch of salt

<u>Procedure</u>

1.  Prepare the salsa first by combing all the ingredients and then set aside in the fridge to chill.

2.  Pre-heat the grill on medium-high temperature.

3.  In small bowl, combine the olive oil, garlic powder, chili flakes, and season with salt and pepper. Stir well.

4. Brush the olive oil mixture on the pork chops and then grill for about 4-5 minutes on each side.

5. Serve along with the salsa on the side.

# *Arugula Salad in Tahini Dressing*

(Serves: 1)

## Ingredients

2 cups arugula

½ cup sliced mushroom

1 cup cooked chicken, diced

1 tsp. olive oil

1 organic egg, boiled and sliced

### For the dressing:

¼ cup tahini

¼ cup extra virgin olive oil

1 juice of lemon

5 cloves of garlic

¼ tsp. Dijon mustard

¼ cup parsley, chopped

1 tsp. honey

1 tsp. anchovy paste

Salt and pepper to taste

(You can store the extra dressing for your other salads)

## Procedure

1.  Place all the ingredients of the dressing in a blender and mix until you achieve a smooth consistency. Set aside.

2.  Meanwhile, heat 1 tsp. of olive oil on a non-stick skillet over medium fire. Sauté the shiitake until they become tender. Season with salt.

3.  Place the shiitake on top of the arugula and drizzle with the tahini dressing. Serve with the cooked egg on the side.

# Chapter 6: Healthy and Delicious Snacks and Shakes You Can Make in a Breeze

If you want your metabolism to run on high almost all day, it's important that you eat 5-6 small meals throughout the day. In between the three main meals, you can have light snacks or shakes that are healthy and easy to make, such as the ones in this chapter.

## *Belly Busting Pomegranate and Berry Smoothie*

Prep time: 5 minutes

Ingredients:

1-cup blueberries (frozen)

1-cup strawberries (frozen)

1 ripe banana (frozen)

1-cup pomegranate

1 cup unsweetened almond milk

You Lean, and Boost Your Metabolism!

Procedure

1. Combine all the ingredients in a blender, and mix until you achieve a smooth consistency.

2. Consume immediately.

## Spiced Green Smoothie

Prep time: 10 minutes

Ingredients:

1 avocado (cut into chunks)

1 ripe banana (frozen)

1 apple (sliced)

2 cups spinach or kale leaves (roughly chopped)

1" ginger root (peeled)

1 cup unsweetened almond milk

1-cup ice cubes

Procedure

1. Combine all the ingredients in a blender, and mix until you achieve a smooth consistency.

2. Consume immediately.

## *Refreshing Smoothie*

Prep time: 5 minutes

Ingredients:

1-cup pineapple chunks (you can use those in can, but drain the syrup)

1 ripe banana (frozen)

½ cup low-fat yogurt

1/3 cup passion fruit concentrate (chilled)

½ cup water

1 tbsp. oats

Procedure

1. Combine all the ingredients in a blender, and mix until you achieve a smooth consistency. (You can add ice cubes if you want)

2. Consume immediately.

## *Peanut Butter and Apple Snacks*

Prep time: 5-8 minutes

Ingredients:

1 large apple (cut into thick slices)

2 tbsp. peanut butter

2 tbsp. raisins

1 tbsp. unsweetened coconut flakes

Procedure

1.  Lay the apple slices on the plate and spread peanut butter over them.

2.  Top with raisins and coconut flakes.

3.  Serve.

## *No-Bake Energy Bars*

Prep time: 10 minutes (needs to be prepared the night before)

Ingredients:

2 cups oats

1-cup peanut butter

½ cup dark chocolate chips

½ cup raisins

½ cup chia seeds

½ cup coconut milk

¼ cup honey

Procedure

1. Place the oats in a food processor and pulse until it turns powder like.

2. Transfer the oats in a bowl and mix together with the dark chocolate chips, raisins, and chia seeds.

3. In a separate bowl, combine the coconut milk, honey, and peanut butter. Mix well.

4. Pour the milk and peanut butter over the oats and mix well until all the ingredients are combined.

5. Spread the oats in a medium-sized baking pan. Cover the pan with aluminum foil and leave inside the fridge overnight.

6. In the morning, slices the oats into bars before consuming.

## *Lettuce Wraps*

Prep time: 12-15 minutes

Ingredients:

6 leaves of butter lettuce

16 oz. chicken fillets (cut into strips)

1 small bell pepper (cut into thin strips)

1 carrot (julienned)

2 cloves of garlic (minced)

1" ginger root (minced)

2 tbsp. olive oil (divided into 2 1 tbsp.)

2 pcs green onions (chopped)

For the dressing:

1/3-cup rice wine vinegar

2 tbsp. sesame oil

2 tbsp. light soy sauce

1 tbsp. toasted sesame seeds

Procedure

1. Heat 1 tbsp. of oil in a large pan over medium fire. Cook the chicken strips for 4-5 minutes, or until the all sides are cooked. Remove from the pan and set aside.

2. Add the remaining oil to the pan and sauté the ginger, bell pepper, and carrots for about 2-3 minutes. Add the garlic and cook for 30 seconds.

3. Prepare the dressing while waiting for the veggies to cook. Simple whisk all the ingredients for the dressing in a small bowl. Set aside.

4. Turn off the heat and place the chicken back to the pan. Drizzle with the prepared dressing and toss to coat all the ingredients.

5. Lay the lettuce cups on a plate and top with the chicken and veggies. Garnish with the chopped green onions.

## *Kale Chips*

Prep time: 15 minutes

Ingredients:

2 cups kale (stems removed, rinsed well)

1 tbsp. olive oil

1 tsp. sea salt

½ tsp. pepper

Procedure

1. Preheat oven at 350F.

2. Place the kale in a baking sheet lined with aluminum foil or parchment paper. Drizzle the leaves with olive oil and season with salt and pepper. Use your hands to toss the kale and coat it with the olive oil

3. Place in the oven to bake for 10-12 minutes.

4. Serve or store in an airtight container.

# Chile Lime and Maple Cinnamon Kettle Corn

*Serves:* 6

## Ingredients

- 1 Tbsp. Coconut Oil

- ⅓ C. Popcorn Kernels

- ¼ C. Unsalted Butter, Divided

- 1 Tsp. Lime Zest

- 1 Tsp. Chile Powder

- ½ Tsp Ground Cumin

- ¼ Tsp. Sea Salt

- 2 Tbsp. Pure Maple Flakes

- ½ Tsp. Pure Vanilla Extract

- ½ Tsp. Ground Allspice, Nutmeg, Cinnamon, And Ginger

## Procedure

1. In a pot with a lid, heat the oil and add the kernels. Cover and cook them, shaking the pot, until the corn has popped, around four minutes. Divide it amongst two bowls.

2. In a pot, melt two tablespoons of butter on low and remove it from the heat. Stir in the lime zest and the juice. Season with the salt, cumin, and Chili powder. Pour it over one of the popcorn bowls and toss to coat.

3. Melt the rest of the butter in a clean pot and add the maple flakes. Cook and stir until the maple flakes have

melted. Remove it from the heat and add the allspice, vanilla, nutmeg, cinnamon, and ginger. Pour this over the second bowl of popcorn. Toss to coat.

# Gooey Mac & Cheese Balls

*Serves:* 20

## Ingredients

- 1 C. Butternut Squash, Peeled And Cubed
- 1 C. Cauliflower Florets
- 13 Oz. Whole-Grain Elbow Macaroni
- 2 Tbsp. Unsalted Butter
- 7 Tbsp. Whole-Wheat Flour, Divided
- 1 C. Whole Milk, Divided
- 1 Tbsp. Dijon Mustard
- ½ Tsp. Pepper
- ¼ Tsp. Salt
- 1 C. Mozzarella Cheese, Shredded
- ½ C. Swiss Cheese, Shredded
- ½ C. Monterey Jack Cheese, Shredded
- ½ Tsp. Smoked Paprika
- ½ Tsp. Cayenne Pepper
- 2 Eggs
- 1 ¾ C. Whole-Wheat Panko Bread Crumbs
- 2 Tbsp. Parmesan Cheese, Grated

## Procedure

1.  Bring a pot of water to a boil and add the cauliflower and squash. Cook until the vegetables are tender, around ten to twelve minutes. Drain and reserve a quarter of a cup of the cooking water. Add the vegetables to the food processor and puree them. With the motor still running on low, add the cooking water and set it all aside.

2.  Grease a nine by thirteen-inch baking dish with cooking spray. In a pot, cook the pasta and drain. Return it to the pot.

3.  In a saucepan, melt the butter. Whisk in two tablespoons of flour and cook for one minute. Whisk in half a cup of milk and cook until the sauce is thickened, about another minute. Stir in the vegetable puree, pepper, salt, and mustard. Remove it from the heat and fold in the cheeses. Pour the sauce over the pasta and stir it to coat. In the pan, spread the pasta and refrigerate it for four hours.

4.  In a pie pan, combine the rest of the flour with the cayenne and paprika. In another dish, whisk the eggs and the half a cup of milk together. In a third dish, mix the breadcrumbs with the parmesan cheese.

5.  Arrange the rack in the oven to the bottom third and preheat the oven to 375 degrees Fahrenheit. Line two baking sheets with parchment paper and use a small ice cream scoop to make the pasta into sixty balls. Roll the balls in the flour mix, egg mix, and then the panko mix. Arrange them on the baking sheet. Discard any leftover flour, egg, or panko mixture. Bake on the upper and lower racks for twenty minutes, switching positions halfway through until they are golden brown and the center are gooey.

# Sweet and Sticky Popcorn Balls

*Serves:* 24

## Ingredients

- 1 Tbsp. Unsalted Butter

- 7 C. Popped Popcorn

- ½ C. Sucanat

- 1 Tsp. Pure Vanilla Extract

- ⅓ C. Unsweetened Dried Cherries, Chopped

- ¼ C. Raw Unsalted Walnuts, Chopped

- ¼ Tsp. Ground Cinnamon

- Pinch Cayenne Pepper

- 1 Oz. 70% Cocoa Dark Chocolate, Melted

- ¼ C. Unsweetened Dried Apricot, Chopped

- ¼ C. C Unsalted Raw Almonds, Chopped

- 2 Tbsp. Pepitas

## Procedure

1. Grease two heatproof bowls with some butter and divide the popcorn amongst the bowls. IN the first bowl add the walnuts, cherries, cayenne, and cinnamon. To the second bowl, add the almonds, apricots, and pepitas. Stir the bowls to combine and line a baking sheet with some waxed paper.

2. In a pan, combine the Sucanat with a quarter of a cup of water. Heat it to medium and cook, without stirring,

until it reaches the soft-ball stage, around six minutes. Remove it from the heat and add a tablespoon of butter and vanilla. Stir it gently.

3. Drizzle this mixture over the bowls of popcorn and stir them to coat. With buttered hands, work with one flavor at a time to form twelve balls of popcorn. Transfer to the baking sheet and drizzle chocolate over the cherry ones.

## Peanut Butter Yogurt Dip

*Serves:* 6

### Ingredients

- ½ C. Greek Yogurt

- ¼ C. Natural Peanut Butter

### Procedure

1. Combine everything in a bowl and refrigerate until you're ready to serve it. Serve with fruits or a vegetable.

## *Classic Cucumber and Tomato Salad*

*Serves:* 5

### Ingredients

- 2 Cucumbers, Peeled And Sliced
- 2 C. Grape Or Cherry Tomatoes, Slice In Half
- ½ Red Onion, Sliced
- ¼ Tsp. Black Pepper
- Kosher Or Sea Salt To Taste
- 2 Tbsp. Fresh Dill
- 2 Tbsp. Balsamic Vinegar
- 1 Tbsp. Extra-Virgin Olive Oil
- 1 Tsp. Dijon Mustard
- 1 Tsp. Honey

### Procedure

1. In a bowl, combine the cucumbers through the onion. Whisk the rest of the ingredients together and pour them over the cucumber salad. Toss to coat and serve.

# Baked Apple Chips

*Serves:* 6

## Ingredients

- 2 Apples, Sliced
- Cinnamon

## Procedure

1. Preheat your oven to 275 degrees Fahrenheit.

2. Line a baking sheet with some parchment paper and put the sliced apple on top.

3. Sprinkle with the cinnamon.

4. Bake for two hours. After an hour, turn them so they bake evenly.

5. Once they're crispy, remove them from the oven and let them cool.

# *Ranch Dip*

*Serves:* 12

## Ingredients

- 1 C. Greek Yogurt

- ½ C. Sour Cream

- 1 Tbsp. Ranch Seasoning

## Procedure

1. Combine the ingredients in a bowl and store in an airtight container in your refrigerator. Allow it to rest overnight before using.

# Sweet Potato Hummus

*Serves:* 10

## Ingredients

- 1 C. Sweet Potatoes, Peeled And Chopped
- 19 Oz. Chickpeas, Rinsed And Drained
- 2 Tbsp. Lemon Juice
- ¼ C. Tahini
- 1 Tbsp. Extra Virgin Olive Oil
- 5 Garlic Cloves, Roasted
- ½ Tsp. Cumin
- Water
- 1 Tsp. Salt

## Procedure

1. Steam the sweet potatoes until they're soft.

2. Transfer the potatoes to a food processor, add the chickpeas through the salt and add two tablespoons of water to start with.

3. Pulse until it's smooth and scrape down the sides. Add water if it's too thick.

4. Adjust your seasonings and serve with a little drizzle of olive oil. Season with paprika and serve.

# Chili Lime Spiced Pumpkin Seeds

*Serves:* 6

## Ingredients

- 2 C. Pumpkin Seeds

- 1 Tbsp. Hot Sauce

- ½ Tbsp. Chili Powder

- 2 Tsp. Lime Juice

- Salt

## Procedure

1. Rinse the seeds in a colander and spread on a baking sheet. Allow them to dry for an hour. Pat them dry with paper towels to save time.

2. Preheat your oven to 275 degrees Fahrenheit.

3. Toss the seeds in the remaining ingredients and put them back on the sheet. Cook for twenty minutes. Remove them from the oven and allow them to cool.

# Sweet and Spicy Pecans

*Serves:* 8

## Ingredients

- 1 Lb. Raw Pecan Halves
- 2 Tbsp. Honey
- 1 Tsp. Chili Powder
- ½ Tsp. Salt
- ½ Tsp. Onion Powder
- ¼ Tsp. Garlic Powder
- ½ Tsp. Cayenne Pepper

## Procedure

1. Combine the ingredients in a slow cooker and stir the pecans to coat them with the honey and the spices.
2. Cover and cook on high for fifteen minutes.
3. Turn on low and cook for an hour, stirring every fifteen minutes.
4. Transfer to a baking sheet and cool them completely.

# Quinoa Salad with a Zing

(Serves: 2)

## Ingredients

½ cup quinoa

1 ripe avocado, cut into chunks

½ cup cherry tomatoes, sliced in half

½ of a small cucumber, diced

4 tbsp. cilantro, chopped

4 tbsp. lime juice

¼ tsp. cumin

salt to taste

## Procedure

1. Cook the quinoa according to the package instructions.

2. When the quinoa is cooked, place it in a large bowl and carefully combine it with the rest of the ingredients.

3. You can adjust the salt and cumin to your preferred taste.

# Homemade Trail Mix

(Serves: 2-3)


## Ingredients

1 cup almonds

½ cup raw walnuts, chopped

½ cup pumpkin seeds

½ cup sunflower seeds

½ cup raisins

¾ cup coconut flakes, unsweetened


## Procedure

1.  Mix all the ingredients in a bowl. Serve.

2.  You can prepare this trail mix in advance and just store it in an air-tight container.

# *Apple Sandwich*

(Serves: 1)

Ingredients

1 large apple, cut into thick slices

2 tbsp. all-natural peanut butter

2 tbsp. golden raisins

1 tbsp. unsweetened coconut flakes

Procedure

1. Lay half of the apple slices on a plate and generously spread with peanut butter.

2. Top with raisins and sprinkle with coconut flakes and then sandwich with the remaining half of the apple slices.

3. Serve.

# Low-Cal Tuna Salad

(Serves: 2)

## Ingredients

1 can tuna chunks in water (drained)

1 small ripe avocado

4 tbsp. Greek yogurt

¼ tsp. onion powder

¼ tsp. garlic powder

½ tbsp. relish

1 celery stalk, finely chopped

½ onion, finely chopped

2 tbsp. freshly squeezed lemon juice

salt and pepper to taste

a bunch of lettuce, roughly chopped

## Procedure

1. Place the avocado and yogurt in a bowl and mash together. Season with the onion and garlic powder, and then add salt and pepper to taste. Mix well. And then stir in the relish.

2. Add the tuna chunks, celery, and onion and lemon juice. Stir well.

3. Serve the tuna mixture on top of lettuce.

# Mixed Greens Salad

(Serves:3-4)

Ingredients

2 cups kale, chopped

½ cup alfalfa

½ cup broccoli, chopped

½ cup green peas, thawed

1 celery stalk, chopped

1 medium-sized green bell pepper, chopped

1 small cucumber, chopped

1 small zucchini, chopped

1 tsp. extra virgin olive oil

¼ tsp. kosher salt

½ tsp. ground black pepper

½ juice of lemon

Procedure

1. In a salad bowl, place the kale. Season with salt and pepper and drizzle with olive oil. Toss the ingredients together and let it sit for about 3 minutes.

2. Add the rest of the ingredients, including the lemon juice. Stir well.

3.  Serve.

## *Asian Broccoli Salad*

(Serves: 2)

Ingredients

2-3 cups broccoli florets, roughly chopped

1 pc. carrot, grated

¼ cup cranberries, chopped

1 tbsp. low-sodium soy sauce

½ tbsp. honey

1 tbsp. rice wine vinegar

¼ cup extra virgin olive oil

¼ tsp. ginger, minced

¼ tsp. garlic powder

2 tbsp. sesame seeds, lightly toasted

Procedure

1. In a small bowl combine the soy sauce, honey, rice wine vinegar, olive oil, ginger, and garlic. Mix well.

2. In a bigger bowl, place the broccoli florets, cranberries, and carrots and the drizzle with the mixture. Toss the salad making sure the veggies are coated with the dressing.

3. Allow the flavors to mix together by letting the salad sit for about 30 minutes.

4.  Top with sesame seeds on top before serving.

## *Kale and Beet Salad*

(Serves: 4-5)

Ingredients

1 pc. beet, boiled, peeled and cut into strips

1 bowl of kale, trimmed and cut into strips

1 small cucumber, diced

1 ripe avocado, cut into cubes

½ cup walnuts, chopped

1 cup raspberries

4 tbsp. hemp seeds

**For the dressing:**

¼ cup white wine vinegar

¼ cup freshly squeezed orange juice

1 tbsp. orange zest

2 tsp. honey

½ tbsp. shallots, minced

sea salt to taste

4 tbsp. extra virgin olive oil

Procedure

1. Combine all the ingredients of the dressing in a small bowl. Whisk well.

2. Place the kale on a huge salad bowl and pour the dressing over the leaves. Toss well allowing the kale to absorb the mixture. Allow to sit for 30 minutes to an hour to make the kale a bit less tough.

3. Add the beets, cucumber, avocado, and raspberries, with the kale and mix well.

4. Serve with walnuts and hemp seeds on top.

## *Sweet and Savory Salad*

(Serves: 2)

Ingredients

1 cup ripe mango, chopped

1 cup ripe avocado, chopped

½ cup black beans, rinsed

½ cup corn kernels

1 small red bell pepper, chopped

1 tomato, chopped

1 small red onion, finely chopped

¼ cup fresh cilantro, chopped

4 tbsp. lime juice

salt to taste

Procedure

1.  Combine all ingredients in a bowl and carefully toss to coat the ingredients with the lime juice.

2.  For better taste, allow the salad to sit covered in the fridge for at least an hour to allow the flavors to marry.

# Cabbage Salad

(Serves: 2-3)

Ingredients

2 cups cabbage, chopped

1 pc. carrot, shredded

1 small apple, chopped

1 cup green peas, thawed

½ green onion, chopped

½ cup slivered almonds

salt to taste

**For the dressing:**

½ juice of lemon

1 tbsp. rice wine vinegar

½ cup extra virgin olive oil

salt to taste

Procedure

1. Whisk all the dressing ingredients in a salad bowl and then add the vegetables, peas, and apples on top. Season with salt and toss well. Let the salad sit for at least 30 minutes in the fridge.

2. Add the slivered almonds on top before serving.

# *Watermelon Salad*

(Serves: 1)

## Ingredients

2 cups watermelon, cut into cubes

½ cup blackberries

2 tbsp. fresh basil leaves, finely chopped

2-3 tbsp. juice of lime

1 tbsp. maple syrup

## Procedure

1. Carefully mix all the ingredients in a bowl. Set aside in the fridge for about 30 minutes before serving.

2. Enjoy.

# Chapter 7 – Tasty Desserts

Who doesn't like dessert? Keep it to a minimum and eat dessert two to three times a week, and use one of these recipes for your next indulgence!

## *Mocha Cashew Bars*

*Serves:* 12

Ingredients

- 1 C. Old-Fashioned Rolled Oats

- 18 Pitted Dates

- 1 ½ C. Puffed Kamut

- ⅓ C. Roasted, Unsalted Cashews

- 1 Tsp. Espresso Powder

- ½ Tsp Sea Salt, Divided

- ½ Tsp Pure Vanilla Extract

- ¼ C. Unsalted Cashew Butter

- 1 Oz. 70% Dark Chocolate, Chopped

## Procedure

1. Cut the parchment paper to cover the bottom and halfway up the sides of an eight by eight baking dish.

2. Heat a pot on high and add the oats to toast for two minutes. Transfer them to a food processor and return the pot to the stove. Add the dates and two tablespoons of water. Cover with a lid and bring to a simmer. Then turn off the heat and allow it to steam for five minutes.

3. Add the Kamut, cashews, a teaspoon of espresso powder, and a quarter of a teaspoon of salt to the food processor. Pulse for two minutes. Add the cashew butter and process for two more minutes.

4. Scrape the date mix into the bowl with the oat mix and work the dry ingredients and date paste together by folding and pushing them together. Knead it for a minute until it comes into a lump.

5. Press into the dish.

6. Stir a pinch of the espresso powder into the melted chocolate and drizzle over the bars. Cover with plastic wrap and refrigerate for an hour. Cut into twelve bars and keep it wrapped and refrigerated for up to five days.

# Chocolate Peanut Squares

*Serves:* 25

## Ingredients

- ½ C. Coconut Sugar, Divided
- ½ C. Brown Rice Flour
- ¼ C. Almond Flour
- ¼ C. Unsweetened Cocoa Powder
- 6 Tbsp. Unsalted Butter, Cubed
- 2 Eggs
- 2 Tbsp. Unsalted Peanut Butter
- 1 Tsp. Pure Vanilla Extract
- ¼ Tsp. Sea Salt
- ¼ C. Unsweetened Shredded Coconut
- ¼ C. Roasted Unsalted Peanuts, Chopped
- ⅓ C. Dark Chocolate Chips

## Procedure

1. Preheat your oven to 350 degrees Fahrenheit. Grease an eight by eight baking dish with some cooking spray and line it with parchment paper. Leave a two-inch overhang on two sides.

2. Prepare the crust by pulsing three tablespoons of the coconut sugar, cocoa powder, and flours together until combined. Add the butter to the food processor and

pulse for another five to seven pulses. Press into the pan and bake for twelve minutes.

3.  In a bowl, use a mixer to beat the peanut butter, eggs, vanilla, salt, and remaining sugar together until fluffy and doubled in two to three minutes. Beat in the coconut and spread the mixture over the crust.

4.  Bake for eight minutes.

5.  Top with the peanuts and chocolate chips and bake another three to five minutes.

6.  Cool on a wire rack and transfer to a cutting board. Cut into twenty-five squares.

# Lemon, Coconut and Cayenne Mousse

*Serves:* 8

## Ingredients

- 3 Eggs

- 1 ½ Tbsp. Lemon Zest, Divided

- ½ C. Lemon Juice, Divided

- ½ C. Pure Maple Syrup

- ¼ C. Coconut Oil

- 2 13.5 Oz. Coconut Milk, Refrigerated Overnight

- ¼ Tsp. Cayenne Pepper

## Procedure

1. In a pot, whisk the eggs, lemon zest, and maple syrup together. Set it on medium heat and whisk until it turns pale yellow and creamy, around five minutes. To the pan, alternate adding the coconut oil and the lemon juice a bit at a time. Whisk until the mix is creamy and the color is even. Bubbles to begin to form.

2. Remove it from the heat and pour it through a sieve into a bowl. Press to be sure the mixture gets through. Cover and refrigerate for four hours or overnight.

3. Just before you serve, remove the cans from the refrigerator and open them from the bottom. Pour out the water and reserve it for another use. Scoop the white cream into a metal bowl and add the cayenne. Beat with an electric beater for thirty seconds or until it's creamy. Fold into the lemon mixture and serve.

# *Date and Cashew Protein Balls*

*Serves:* 24

## Ingredients

- ¾ C. Raw Unsalted Cashews

- 10 Dates, Pitted

- ½ C. Unsweetened Cacao Powder

- 1 Tsp. Hemp Seeds

## Procedure

1. Soak the cashews in a quarter of a cup of water for ten minutes.

2. Add the cashews to the food processor with the water, and then add the remaining ingredients. Process until it makes a dough, around two minutes.

3. Remove it from the food processor and make twenty-four balls. Roll in some additional cacao powder.

4. Refrigerate for twenty minutes before serving.

# Chestnut Crusted Cheesecake with Cranberry Sauce

*Serves:* 12

## Ingredients

- 1 C. Peeled Roasted Unsalted Chestnuts
- 3 Tbsp. Almond Meal
- 2 Tbsp. Maple Flakes
- 3 Eggs
- 8 Oz. Cream Cheese
- 1½ C. Ricotta Cheese
- 1 C. Greek Yogurt
- ¾ C. Maple Flakes
- 2 Tsp. Finely Grated Orange Zest
- ¼ C. Fresh Orange Juice
- 1 Tsp. Pure Almond Extract
- 1 Tsp. Pure Vanilla Extract
- 2 C. Frozen Cranberries
- ½ C. Maple Flakes

## Procedure

1. Preheat the oven to 375 degrees Fahrenheit. To prepare the crust, grease a nine-inch springform pan with cooking spray.

2.  In a food processor, grind the chestnuts up. Add the almond meal and two tablespoons of maple flakes. Pulse until it looks like crumbs. Press this into the bottom of the pan and bake for ten minutes. Set it aside and reduce the oven temperature to 325 degrees Fahrenheit.

3.  To prepare the filling, wipe out the bowl of the food processor and add the eggs through the pure vanilla extract. Pulse until it's smooth and pour into the crust. Bake until it's set, around forty-five minutes. To prevent it from cracking, turn off your oven and allow it to come to room temperature in the oven for about an hour.

4.  In the meantime, prepare the topping. In a pot over medium heat, bring the cranberries, half a cup of water, and half a cup of maple flakes to a boil. Reduce the heat to low and simmer until the cranberries burst around three minutes. Drizzle the sauce over the cheesecake and serve.

# Individual Apple and Pecan Crumbles

*Serves:* 10

## Ingredients

- ½ C. White Whole-Wheat Flour

- 2 Tbsp. Unsalted Butter, Diced

- ½ C. Rolled Oats

- 2 Tbsp. Chopped Unsalted Pecans

- ⅓ C. Plus 2 Tbsp. Evaporated Cane Juice, Divided

- ¼ Tsp. Salt, Divided

- 2 ½ Lb. Sweet-Tart Apples Cored, Peeled, And Sliced

- 1 Tbsp. Fresh Lemon Juice

- ¼ C. Crème Fraiche

## Procedure

1. Grease ten half cup ramekins with cooking spray and arrange them on a baking sheet.

2. Prepare the crumble topping by combining the flour and butter in a bowl. Mix it together with a pastry cutter until it looks like a fine meal. Stir in the oats, pecans, a third of a cup of the cane juice, and a quarter of a teaspoon of salt. Set it aside.

3. In a bowl, add the apples, juice, and two tablespoons of the cane juice with a pinch of salt. Transfer the fruit to the ramekins.

4. Preheat the oven to 375 degrees Fahrenheit. Sprinkle the crumble topping on the apples and bake for an hour. Set

it aside to allow it to cool for ten minutes. Top with the crème Fraiche and divide evenly.

# Buttermilk Plum Cake

*Serves:* 12

## Ingredients

- Olive Oil Cooking Spray
- 2 C. Whole-Grain Spelt Flour
- ½ C. Sucanat
- 1 ½ Tsp. Baking Powder
- ¾ Tsp. Ground Cardamom
- 1 Tsp. Ground Cinnamon
- ½ Tsp Sea Salt
- 1 Egg
- 1 ½ C. Buttermilk
- 3 Tbsp. Organic Unsalted Butter, Melted
- ½ Tsp Pure Vanilla Extract
- 3 Black Plums, Sliced

## Procedure

1. Preheat your oven to 350 degrees Fahrenheit. Grease a ten-inch tart pan with cooking spray.

2. In a bowl, mix the Sucanat, flour, cinnamon, baking powder, salt, and cardamom together. In a medium bowl, whisk the buttermilk, egg, vanilla, and butter together. Add the liquid mix to the dry mix and stir to combine.

3.  Add the batter to the prepared pan and smooth the surface. Lay the plums on the surface and bake for forty minutes. Transfer to a wire rack to cool.

# Chapter 8 – More Delicious Shakes and Smoothies

## *Sunshine on a Cup*

(Serves: 2)

Ingredients

1 cup frozen ripe mango, chopped

½ cup almond milk

1 tsp. chia seeds

¼ cup low-fat cottage cheese

1 tsp. maple syrup


Procedure

1. Place all the ingredients in a blender and mix until smooth. Serve immediately.

## *Spiced Apple Shake*

(Serves: 2)

Ingredients

1 cup apple, chopped

1 cup baby spinach

1 cup almond milk, vanilla flavor

½ tsp. cinnamon powder

Procedure

1. Place all the ingredients in a blender and mix until smooth. Serve immediately.

# Coco-Banana Green Shake

(Serves: 2)

## Ingredients

1 cup coconut milk, light

1 ripe banana, frozen

1 cup baby spinach

1 tsp. vanilla extract

2 tbsp. coconut flakes

## Procedure

1. Place all the ingredients in a blender and mix until smooth. Serve immediately.

# *Kale and Berry Shake*

(Serves: 1)


Ingredients

¾ cup frozen blueberries

½ frozen banana

1 cup kale

1 tbsp. all-natural peanut butter

¾ cup almond milk, vanilla flavor


Procedure

1. Place all the ingredients in a blender and mix until smooth. Serve immediately.

# Berrilicious Quinoa Smoothie

(Serves: 2)

## Ingredients

½ cooked quinoa

1 cup frozen strawberries

1 frozen banana

½ cup green tea

ice cubes

## Procedure

1. Place all the ingredients in a blender and mix until smooth. Serve immediately.

## *Pomegranate Smoothie*

(Serves: 2)

Ingredients

1 cup 100% pomegranate juice, unsweetened

1 kiwi, peeled

½ cup Greek yogurt

1 tbsp. all-natural peanut butter

1 tsp. vanilla extract

2 tbsp. flax seeds

Procedure

1. Place all the ingredients in a blender and mix until smooth. Serve immediately.

# Clean Eating Green Shake

(Serves: 2)

<u>Ingredients</u>

1 cup collard greens

1 frozen banana

½ fresh cranberries

¼ cup zucchini, sliced

½ cup coconut milk, light

¼ tsp. allspice

<u>Procedure</u>

1. Place all the ingredients in a blender and mix until smooth. Serve immediately.

# Conclusion

Thank you again for purchasing this book!

Learning about the benefits of clean eating would really encourage you to try out this lifestyle, and I admire your effort to choose to begin this lifestyle in order to become healthy and lose weight. I hope that this book helped you realize that even if you're a beginner in the kitchen, or even if you follow a busy schedule, you can still create healthy meals that you and your family can enjoy. My wish is that you follow the tips I shared with you and create your clean eating meal plans based on the recipes I shared with you in this book.

Thank you, and good luck!

- Jason Green